AMERICAN SCRIPTURES

American Scriptures

BY

Carl Van Doren AND **Carl Carmer**

ILLUSTRATED WITH PICTURES FROM
VARIOUS FAMOUS COLLECTIONS
OF AMERICANA

★

Boni & Gaer • New York • 1946

★

CONTENTS

★

PART TWO: Holidays

PART THREE: *Heroes*

vi

PART SEVEN: Principles

PART EIGHT: The West

LIST OF ILLUSTRATIONS

★

FOREWORD

The *American Scriptures*, here for the first time printed, have been selected from the series originally broadcast for the radio audience during the intermissions of the Sunday concerts of the Philharmonic Symphony Society of New York, from May 1943 through 1944. In that troubled time they were intended to lift the spirits of Americans by recalling to them heroic things done and wise things said in the American past, by men and women who had once lived through other great national emergencies with the faith and fortitude which were now again demanded of the people of this nation. While these historic episodes were set forth in dramatic form, suitable for broadcasting, they were authentic history in the sense that the words quoted were real words, so far as possible, and the actions were accurately reported, not invented. In this the *American Scriptures* differ from most versions of history, on stage, screen, or radio, which take large liberties with the known or knowable facts on the assumption that the truth is not so interesting as fiction. The *American Scriptures* assumed that nothing can be quite so interesting as the truth.

Most of them were written by the authors represented in this collection, in about the proportions in which they here appear. The general aim of the series was to move through the whole of American history, though not chronologically, and over the whole of American geography at home or abroad, though not too systematically. There was not time enough to carry out the entire plan. But it will be seen that the materials cover a very wide range under the different heads of Statesmen, Holidays, Heroes, Family Letters, Opening of the Continent, Monuments, Principles, The West, and Songs. Among them they throw light on most of what is essential in American history, character, and aspira-

Edmund Burke and
Patrick Henry

THERE are two American Scriptures which are really one. They are really both American, though one of them was spoken by an Irish member of the British House of Commons. What he said on March 22, 1775, in London, belongs forever with what a Virginian said only a day later in that same year, three thousand miles away.

On that March 22, 1775, Edmund Burke made his great speech on the need of conciliation between the stubborn Parliament and the restless colonies in North America.

And this is how Burke described the character of the Americans.

★

In this character of the Americans, a love of freedom is the predominating feature which marks and distinguishes the whole; and as an ardent is always a *jealous* affection, your colonies become suspicious, restive, and untractable, whenever they see the least attempt to wrest from them by force, or shuffle from them by chicane, what they think the only advantage worth living for. This fierce spirit of liberty is stronger in the English colonies probably than in any other people of the earth. . . . .

In other countries, the people, more simple and of a less mercurial cast, judge of an ill principle in government only by an actual grievance; here they anticipate the evil, and judge of the pressure of the grievance by the badness of the principle. They augur misgovernment at a distance and snuff the approach of tyranny in every tainted breeze . . . .

To prove that the Americans ought not to be free, we are obliged to depreciate the value of freedom itself; and we never seem to gain a paltry advantage over them in debate without attacking some of those principles, or deriding some of those feelings, for which our ancestors have shed their blood . . . .

We cannot, I fear, falsify the pedigree of this fierce people, and persuade them that they are not sprung from a nation in whose veins the blood of freedom circulates . . . . An Englishman is the unfittest person on earth to argue another Englishman into slavery.

What Burke had said in London was to be confirmed in Richmond, Virginia, within twenty-four hours.

St. John's Church, in Richmond on the hill that overlooks the town and the James River, was packed with troubled men. There were more than a hundred of them — delegates whom the counties of Virginia had sent to this convention.

The most eminent names in Virginia were represented here: there was the brilliant young thinker from Albermarle County, Thomas Jefferson. There was the blond, ruddy, silent planter from Fairfax County, George Washington.

STATESMEN

There was the delegate from Hanover County, Patrick Henry. In the pulpit was Peyton Randolph, president of the convention.

The room was tense with feeling and hot with debate. Every man there believed that the government in London was steadily encroaching upon the right of the Americans to have a say in how they should be governed.

Patrick Henry, tall, lean, dark, eagle-faced, not yet forty but known throughout Virginia for his eloquent pleading at the bar, had no doubt what the next step should be. He proposed an uncompromising resolution: let Virginia arm itself against further encroachment. The time for humble protests was past. There was a storm of argument.

Jefferson outspokenly agreed with Henry. Washington did not speak, but there was agreement in his eyes. Conservative delegates opposed the resolution: for Virginia to arm itself was to go beyond politics into civil war, they pleaded. Let us keep the peace. Let us go on hoping for reconciliation.

And now, in the midst of this debate, Patrick Henry rose to cut across it in words on fire with the spirit of liberty that Burke had described only the day before. The fulfillment of Burke's prophecy had come almost as swiftly as an echo:

*

Mr. President, it is natural to man to indulge in the illusions of hope. We are apt to shut our eyes against a painful truth, and listen to the song of the siren, till she transforms us into

4

beasts. Is this the part of wise men, engaged in a great and arduous struggle for liberty? . . . .

Let us not, I beseech you, Sir, deceive ourselves longer. Sir, we have done everything that could be done to avert the storm which is now coming on. We have petitioned; we have remonstrated; we have supplicated; we have prostrated ourselves . . . . Our petitions have been slighted; our remonstrances have produced additional violence and insult; our supplications have been disregarded; and we have been spurned with contempt from the foot of the throne. In vain, after these things, may we indulge the fond hope of peace and reconciliation.

There is no longer any room for hope. If we wish to be free . . . . we must fight! I repeat, Sir, we must fight! An appeal to arms and to the God of Hosts is all that is left to us.

They tell us, Sir, that we are weak; unable to cope with so formidable an adversary. But when shall we be stronger? Will it be the next week, or the next year? . . . . Shall we gather strength by irresolution and inaction? . . . .

Sir, we are not weak, if we make a proper use of the means which the God of Nature hath placed in our power. Three millions of people, armed in the holy cause of liberty, and in such a country as that which we possess, are invincible by any force which our enemy can send against us . . . . The battle, Sir, is not to the strong alone, it is to the vigilant, the active, the brave. Besides, Sir, we have no election. If we were base enough to desire it, it is now too late to retire from the contest. There is no retreat but in submission and slavery! Our chains are forged! Their clanking may be heard on the plains of Boston! THE WAR IS INEVITABLE; AND LET IT COME! I REPEAT IT, SIR, LET IT COME! ! !

It is in vain, Sir, to extenuate the matter. Gentlemen may cry peace, peace, peace — but there is no peace. The war is actually begun! The next gale that sweeps from the North will bring to our ears the clash of resounding arms! Our brethren are already in the field! Why stand we here idle? What is it that Gentlemen wish? What would they have? Is life so dear, or peace so sweet, as to be purchased at the price of chains and slavery? Forbid it, Almighty God! I know not what course others may take; but as for me, GIVE ME LIBERTY, OR GIVE ME DEATH!

Within a month after these speeches by Edmund Burke and Patrick Henry their countries were at war. That war, which ended in the political separation of the United States from the British Empire, increased the love of liberty in both countries. That love was the same in Burke and Henry. It was the same in the English-speaking peoples on both sides of the Atlantic. It is still the same — and it is their greatest gift to mankind.

★ 2 ★

Franklin and the Constitution

WE THINK now of the Constitution of the United States as foursquare and tough and flexible and enduring. We have lived under it all our lives. But in September 1787 the Constitution was a new and yet untried scheme of government. The men gathered in Independence Hall in Philadelphia had been working on it for four months. There had been quarrels that almost broke up the Convention. These were all sorts of men, from all parts of the country: New Englanders, Southern plantation owners, Pennsylvanians. Government, to each one of them, meant compromise, conflict, security, liberty — in many varying degrees.

On this morning the final reading of the Constitution had just ended. The high, historic room was silent.

The tall, grave man in the president's chair on the dais was George Washington of Virginia. Above his head, on the high back of his chair, a rising sun was painted.

On the floor the oldest member of the Convention rose to his feet. His merry blue eys looked out through the bifocal glasses that he himself had invented. This, of course, was Benjamin Franklin of Philadelphia. And of Paris. And of London. And of the World. The time had come to sign the Constitution. Yet there were some in that hall who, even

7

then, could not tell what action they would take. Franklin, facing this room full of famous men, rallied them as soldiers on the fighting line.

George Washington recognized the delegate from Pennsylvania, and Franklin, standing, let his greatest speech be read for him by young James Wilson, also of Pennsylvania:

*

Mr. President: I confess that there are several parts of this Constitution which I do not at present approve; but I am not sure I shall never approve them, for, having lived long, I have experienced many instances of being obliged, by better information or fuller consideration, to change opinions even on important subjects which I once thought right, but found to be otherwise. It is therefore that the older I grow the more apt I am to doubt my own judgment, and pay more respect to the judgment of others. . . . .

In these sentiments, Sir, I agree to this Constitution, with all its faults, if they are such . . . . I doubt too whether any other Convention we can obtain may be able to make a better Constitution. For when you assemble a number of men to have the advantage of their joint wisdom, you inevitably assemble with those men all their prejudices, their passions, their errors of opinion, their local interests, and their selfish views. From such an assembly can a perfect production be expected? It therefore astonishes me, Sir, to find this system approaching so near to perfection as it does; and I think it will astonish our enemies, who are waiting with confidence to hear that our councils are confounded, like those of the builders of Babel . . . . Thus I consent, Sir, to this Constitution because I expect no better, and because I am not sure that it is not the best. The opinions I have had of its errors I sacrifice to the public good. I have never whispered a syllable of them abroad. Within these walls they were born, and here they shall die . . . . I hope therefore that for our own sakes, as part of the people, and for the sake of posterity, we shall act heartily and unanimously in recommending this Constitution . . . . wherever our influence may extend, and turn our future thoughts and endeavours to the means of having it well administered.

On the whole, Sir, I cannot help expressing a wish that every member of this Convention, who may still have objections to it would with me on this occasion doubt a little of his own infallibility, and, to make manifest our unanimity, put his name to this instrument.

While the delegates were signing, Franklin looked at the sun painted on the back of the President's chair. And he said:

★

I have often, in the course of the session, looked at that sun behind the President, without being able to tell whether it was rising or setting. But now, at length, I have the happiness to know that it is a rising and not a setting sun.

★ 3 ★
Jefferson's Inaugural Address

On March 4, 1801 Washington was not a city except in name and in hope. The Capitol and the White House were still unfinished. Pennsylvania Avenue, leading from one to the other, was a muddy road through an alder swamp. The town, what there was of it, looked less like a nation's capital than like a raw and not too prosperous real estate development.

But there was an idea back of this. The new nation wanted a new capital to grow up, as people said, with the country. And now the people had elected a new president who seemed to them to face the future as the new Capitol did.

He was Thomas Jefferson, who had written the Declaration of Independence twenty-five years before. Jefferson still believed that all men were created equal.

A good many Americans had in 1801 come to believe that this was a mere theory. The Federalists, the party in power, had recently seemed to be more interested in making the government strong than in keeping the people free. They had passed laws abridging the rights of free speech and a free press. But the people, resenting this, had overwhelmed the Federalists in the recent presidential election. A new people's party had elected Jefferson, the Republican (later Democratic) Party's founder and leader.

Jefferson's Inaugural Address

John Adams, the retiring President, was so much chagrined that he could not bear to see his successor inaugurated. Adams had slipped out of Washington in his coach at four o'clock that morning.

Across the square from the Capitol, on this bright March 4, 1801, was Conrad's boarding-house, where Jefferson lived. A company of militia artillery was drawn up in front of the door.

At noon Jefferson came out with a few friends. He was very tall and slender. His reddish hair was beginning to turn gray. He was plainly dressed in an ordinary coat, with green knee-breeches and gray woolen stockings. To the sound of guns fired by the artillery company, he walked with a lounging, unceremonious gait across the square to the completed north wing of the Capitol, where the Senate was sitting.

The senators were there, and the members of the House of Representatives had come in from their temporary quarters. The newly-elected Vice-President, Aaron Burr of New York, as president of the Senate, was in the chair. At his left sat John Marshall of Virginia, newly appointed Chief Justice of the United States Supreme Court. Marshall and Burr heartily disliked each other. Both disliked Jefferson, and Jefferson disliked both of them. But today Burr courteously gave up the vice-president's chair to Jefferson, and took another seat at his right . . . .

The Senate Chamber was full of animosities. Party spirit was still high and hot, after a campaign fought with terrible bitterness, political and personal. To many, the election of Jefferson seemed very close to a second revolution. The Federalists present were convinced that the government of their country had passed into the control of the rabble, led by a demagogue, and the new party had still to prove that they could safeguard liberty and yet prevent disorder.

In the circumstances, Jefferson was expected to speak like a triumphant and scornful revolutionary. But it was no partisan speech that the new chief executive made. He spoke merely as an American to and for all Americans:

*

Friends and Fellow-Citizens:
Called upon to undertake the duties of the first executive office of our country, I avail myself of the presence of that portion of my fellow-citizens which is here assembled, to express my grateful thanks for the favor with which they have been pleased to look toward me. . . .

During the contest of opinion through which we have passed, the animation of discussions and of exertions has sometimes worn an aspect which might impose on strangers unused to think freely and to speak and write what they think; but this being now decided by the voice of the nation, announced according to the rules of the Constitution, all will, of course, arrange themselves under the will of the law, and unite in common efforts for the common good. All, too, will bear in mind this sacred principle, that though the will of the majority is in all cases to prevail, that will to be rightful must be reasonable; that the minority possess their equal rights, which equal law must protect, and to violate would be oppression. Let us, then, fellow-citizens, unite with one heart and one mind. Let us restore to social intercourse that harmony and affection without which liberty and even life itself are but dreary things . . . .

But every difference of opinion is not a difference of principle. We have called by different names brethren of the same principle. We are all Republicans, we are all Federalists . . . .

I know, indeed, that some honest men fear that a republican government cannot be strong, that this Government is not strong enough; but would the honest patriot, in the full tide of successful experiment, abandon a government which has so far kept us free and firm on the theoretic and visionary fear that this Government, the world's best hope, may by possibility want energy to preserve itself? I trust not. I believe this, on the contrary, the strongest Government on earth. I believe it the only one where every man, at the call of the law, would fly to the standard of the law, and would meet invasions of the public order as his own personal concern . . . .

Let us, then, with courage and confidence pursue our own Federal and Republican principles, our attachment to union and representative government . . . .

These principles form the bright constellation which has gone before us and guided our steps through an age of revolution and reformation. The wisdom of our sages and the blood of our heroes have been devoted to their attainment. They should be the creed of our political faith, the text of civic instruction, the touchstone by which to try the services of those we trust; and should we wander from them in moments of error or of alarm, let us hasten to retrace our steps and to regain the road which alone leads to peace, liberty, and safety.

STATESMEN

I repair, then, fellow-citizens, to the post you have assigned me . . . . I ask so much confidence only as may give firmness and effect to the legal administration of your affairs. I shall often go wrong through defect of judgment. When right, I shall often be thought wrong by those whose positions will not command a view of the whole ground. I ask your indulgence for my own errors, which will never be intentional, and your support against the errors of others, who may condemn what they would not if seen in all its parts . . . .

Relying, then, on the patronage of your good will, I advance with obedience to the work, ready to retire from it whenever you become sensible how much better choice is in your power to make. And may that Infinite Power which rules the destinies of the universe lead our councils to what is best, and give them a favorable issue for your peace and prosperity.

When Thomas Jefferson ended his address, he turned to Chief Justice Marshall, who administered the oath of office. Then without any further ceremony, Jefferson walked with his friends back across the square to his boarding-house.

There is no use claiming that Jefferson's wise words about unity of spirit did away with party politics. The country during his administration was very much alive, very much divided on national aims and on the best means of achieving them. Where there is life in a democracy, there is difference of opinion. But the American government under Jefferson continued to be free and firm, in spite of disagreements among its citizens.

14

Jefferson's Inaugural Address

For when Jefferson said: "We are all Republicans, we are all Federalists," he was saying only what we are still saying: We are all Americans.

*Under our free institutions . . . the
people . . . are too enlightened not to
understand their own rights and interests.*

— ANDREW JACKSON

We hold these truths to be self-evident.

18

*I have the happiness to know that it is
a rising and not a setting sun.*
— BENJAMIN FRANKLIN

PLATE THREE
AU GENIE DU FRANKLIN
DRAWN AND ENGRAVED BY FRAGONARD. COURTESY OF THE
METROPOLITAN MUSEUM OF ART, NEW YORK CITY.

21

*Truth and reason
for their guide.*

PLATE FOUR

THE DECLARATION
OF INDEPENDENCE

PAINTED BY JOHN TRUMBULL,

COURTESY OF THE

YALE UNIVERSITY ART GALLERY,

NEW HAVEN, CONNECTICUT.

KEY TO DECLARATION OF INDEPENDENCE
BY JOHN TRUMBULL

1. Gorge Wythe.
2. William Whipple.
3. Joseph Bartlett.
4. Thomas Lynch.
5. Benjamin Harrison.
6. Richard Henry Lee.
7. Samuel Adams.
8. George Clinton.
9. William Paca.
10. Samuel Chase.
11. Richard Stockton.
12. Lewis Morris.
13. William Floyd.
14. Arthur Middleton.
15. Thomas Heyward, Jr
16. Charles Carroll.
17. Robert Morris.
18. Thomas Willing.
19. Benjamin Rush.
20. Elbridge Gerry.
21. Robert Treat Pine.
22. William Hooper.
23. Stephen Hopkins.
24. William Ellery.
25. George Clymer.
26. Joseph Hewes.
27. George Walton.
28. James Wilson.
29. Abraham Clark.
30. Francis Hopkinson.
31. John Adams.
32. Roger Sherman.
33. Robert R. Livingston
34. Thomas Jefferson.
35. Benjamin Franklin.
36. Thomas Nelson, Jr.
37. Francis Lewis.
38. John Witherspoon.
39. Samuel Huntington.
40. William Williams.
41. Oliver Wolcott.
42. Charles Thomson.
43. John Hancock.
44. George Read.
45. John Dickinson.
46. Edward Rutledge.
47. Thomas McKean.
48. Philip Livingston.

23

The American Scriptures tell one great Christmas story.

PLATE FIVE

WASHINGTON CROSSING THE DELAWARE

STUDY BY EMMANUEL LEUTZE, FROM THE COLLECTION OF THE NATIONAL GALLERY OF ART,
WASHINGTON, D. C., BY COURTESY OF HALL PARK MC CULLOUGH.

24

Let us, then, . . . pursue our Federal and Republican principles . . . The wisdom of our sages and the blood of our heroes have been devoted to their attainment.

—THOMAS JEFFERSON

PLATE SIX

WASHINGTON AND HIS GENERALS AT YORKTOWN

PAINTED BY CHARLES WILLSON PEALE. COURTESY OF THE MARYLAND HISTORICAL SOCIETY, BALTIMORE, MARYLAND

*The lessons contained in this valuable
legacy of Washington . . . should be
cherished in the heart of every citizen.*
— ANDREW JACKSON

PLATE SEVEN

FEDERAL HALL,
WALL STREET, NEW YORK
INAUGURATION OF
WASHINGTON, 1789

ENGRAVED BY AMOS DOOLITTLE. FROM THE PHELPS STOKES
COLLECTION. COURTESY OF THE NEW YORK PUBLIC LIBRARY,
NEW YORK CITY.

28

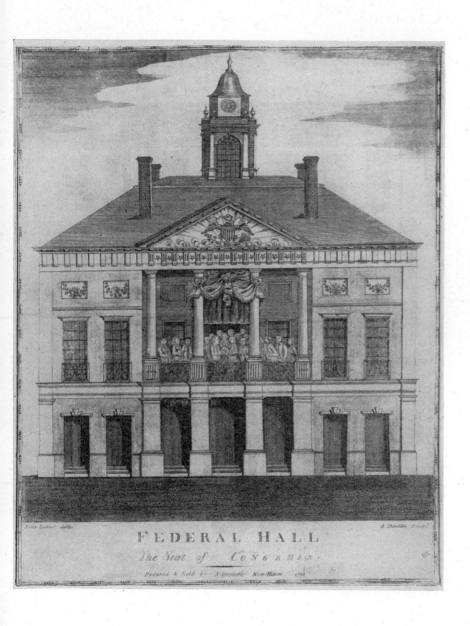

FEDERAL HALL
The Seat of CONGRESS.
Printed & Sold by A. Doolittle New-Haven 1790

29

Equality of rights, embodied in general self-government is the great moral element in modern democracy.

— CARL SCHURZ

PLATE EIGHT

CAPITOL OF THE UNITED STATES AT WASHINGTON

AQUATINT BY SUTHERLAND. FROM THE PHELPS STOKES COLLECTION. COURTESY OF THE NEW YORK PUBLIC LIBRARY, NEW YORK CITY.

30

31

★ 4 ★

Andrew Jackson's Farewell Address

O N THE cold raw fourth of March 1837, twenty thousand people were crowded in front of the Capitol in Washington — as yet no dome towered over it — to see a new president inaugurated.

Or rather, they had come to see the old president retire from office — General Andrew Jackson, Old Hickory. For once, a senator observed, the rising was eclipsed by the setting sun. The new president was merely another president. But the old one was a hero to the nation. As a soldier he had fought many battles, and magnificently won the greatest of them. The first President ever elected from the frontier beyond the Alleghenies, he had throughout his stormy administration had the support of the new democratic America that was rising into power.

For months — as all Washington knew — Jackson had been a sick man. He might not be able to attend today's ceremonies. But about noon he left the White House, riding in a carriage made of wood taken from the hull of that famous old frigate, the *Constitution* — Old Ironsides conveying Old Hickory. The four gray horses known as the Jackson grays drew that carriage. In it sat two men. One, tough, weathered,

33

lean and tall — Old Hickory. The other, suave, elegant, something of a dandy — Martin Van Buren.

The people along muddy, unpaved, ragged Pennsylvania Avenue were quiet. They stood uncovered as their hero went by. The crowd in front of the Capitol was silent, too, when Jackson got out of his carriage at the foot of the long flight of steps. Bareheaded, he moved up to the portico, lean and tall above his companions, his white hair like a crest.

He sat in the portico while Martin Van Buren took the oath of office and delivered his inaugural address, and then descended the broad steps to the waiting carriage.

As if at a signal, the crowd burst into a tumult of affection which the observant senator saw as the acclaim of posterity breaking from the bosoms of contemporaries. Midway in his slow descent Andrew Jackson stopped, took off his hat and bowed his white, proud head to the people. Suddenly this crowd, too, was silent. Jackson entered his carriage and drove away.

He had not spoken a word. Yet by evening the whole city of Washington was reading his Farewell Address to the People of the United States — an address he had written to be printed and distributed that day. Many persons who read his address heard a soldier's and a statesman's voice speaking in the language of a prophet.

Jackson believed, of course, that he was counselling Americans to beware of the danger that lay closest to them: the fierce dissension that threatened the union of the states. He

could not then foresee a time when foreign enemies would do
their best to stir up discord among us . . . to cast doubt on the
good faith of our allies . . . to promote racial and religious
prejudices among our people . . . to destroy the unity of
our national spirit.

Nor could he foresee that some short-sighted and a few
bad-hearted Americans would listen to those artful, designing
enemies. Yet Andrew Jackson's words of farewell might
almost have been uttered yesterday — or today:

★

Fellow-citizens . . . . The necessity of watching with jealous
anxiety for the preservation of the Union was earnestly
pressed upon his fellow-citizens by the Father of his Country
in his Farewell Address. He has there told us that " . . . . there
will always be reason to distrust the patriotism of those who
in any quarter may endeavor to weaken its bands;" . . . .

The lessons contained in this valuable legacy of Washington to his countrymen should be cherished in the heart of
every citizen to the latest generation; and perhaps at no
period of time could they be more usefully remembered than
at the present moment . . . . We behold systematic efforts
publicly made to sow the seeds of discord . . . . Mutual sus-
picions and reproaches may in time create mutual hostility,
and artful and designing men will always be found who are
ready to foment these fatal divisions . . . .

What have you to gain by division and dissensions? . . . .
If these subversive elements should succeed . . . . this great
and glorious Republic would soon be broken up into a

multitude of petty States, without commerce . . . . harassed with conflicts and humbled and debased in spirit, they would be ready to submit to the absolute domination of any militaristic adventurer and to surrender our liberty for the sake of repose . . . .

Rest assured that the men found busy in this work of discord are not worthy of your confidence, and deserve your strongest condemnation.

Under our free institutions, I am sure the people in every part of the United States are too enlightened not to understand their own rights and interests, and to detect and defeat every effort to gain undue advantages over them . . . .

In presenting to you, my fellow-citizens, these parting counsels, I have brought before you the leading principles upon which I endeavored to administer the Government in the high office with which you twice honored me. Knowing that the path of freedom is continually beset by enemies who often assume the disguise of friends, I have devoted the last hours of my public life to warn you of the dangers. The progress of the United States under our free and happy institutions has surpassed the most sanguine hopes of the founders of the Republic . . . . It is from within, among yourselves — from cupidity, from corruption, from disappointed ambition and inordinate thirst for power — that factions will be formed and liberty endangered. It is against such designs, whatever disguise the actors may assume, that you have especially to guard yourselves. You have the highest of human trusts committed to your care. Providence has showered on this favored land blessings without number and has chosen you as the guardians of freedom, to preserve it for the benefit of the human race. May He . . . . enable you . . . . to guard and defend to the end of time the great charge He has committed to your keeping.

Andrew Jackson's Farewell Address

My own race is nearly run; advanced age and failing health warn me that before long I must pass beyond the reach of human events and cease to feel the vicissitudes of human affairs. I thank God that my life has been spent in a land of liberty .... I bid you a last and affectionate farewell.

★ 5 ★
The Gettysburg Address

FOR the best known and best loved of all our American Scriptures, let us go back to the little Pennsylvania town of Gettysburg on a chilly November day in 1863, and try to imagine we are actually there on that great occasion.

It is Thursday, the nineteenth of the month, and ten o'clock in the morning. We are on Cemetery Hill, south of the town, in the new National Cemetery where the soldiers of many states have been buried, state by state, after the bloody battle of July in which nearly a third of all the men on both sides were killed, wounded, or missing at the end of three terrible days of fighting.

The graves are in ordered rows, but the grass has not yet had time to cover them. They look cold and raw, and we shiver as we think of the silent multitude under this solemn ground.

People stream into the cemetery on foot, on horseback, in carriages and wagons. They move about, grieving or curious, among the graves. They gather round the temporary wooden platform built for the speakers in this ceremony of dedication.

Now we hear minute guns fired in the town, and bands playing. The official procession is on its way. It arrives, passing lines of troops drawn up in salute. There are governors of states, members of Congress and of the cabinet, foreign diplomats, generals — and the President of the United States, Abraham Lincoln.

The tall President, riding on a chestnut horse that is said to be the largest in the Cumberland valley, towers in black clothes and high hat above all the others, bowing right and left in response to the cheers. The speakers and guests dismount and go up the steps to the platform.

There is more music from the bands, and the chaplain of the House of Representatives opens the services with a prayer. Then Edward Everett, who has been United States senator, governor of Massachusetts, secretary of state, ambassador to Great Britain, and president of Harvard — Everett, who is considered the foremost orator of his time, — delivers the oration on which he has been working for two months. It is lofty and dignified, with all the finest qualities of classical oratory. It lasts two hours.

Abraham Lincoln, President of the United States, sits waiting. There are many here who hate him; others who think him a western clown who has merely happened into his high office. The committee which planned the dedication services had at first not even thought of asking him to speak. They supposed he was too busy with the war still tearing the nation. They were not sure he could rise to this weighty and sad occasion. And they finally asked him to make only a few remarks, after the main oration, in which he was, as chief executive, formally to set apart the grounds to their sacred use.

The most burdened man in America, he has had no time to write out a long address. He wrote a draft of what he was to say, or notes for it, in Washington ten days or so before, and perhaps he made some changes on the train, coming to Gettysburg yesterday. He finished his speech late last night, and he has it in his pocket. Now Edward Everett has come to his peroration:

*

Friends, let me again, as we part, invoke your benediction on these honored graves . . . . You feel that it was greatly auspicious that the men of nineteen states stood side by side on the perilous ridges of the battle. The spots on which they stood and fell — these pleasant heights; the fertile plain beneath them; the fields beyond the ridge; the little streams which wind through the hills, on whose banks, in aftertimes, the wondering plowmen will turn up, with the rude weapons of savage warfare, the fearful missiles of modern artillery; Seminary Ridge, the Peach Orchard, Cemetery, Culp, and Wolf Hills, Round Top, Little Round Top — humble names, henceforward dear and famous; no lapse of time, no distance of space, shall cause you to be forgotten. "The whole earth," said Pericles, as he stood over the remains of his fellow-countrymen who had fallen in the first years of the Peloponnesian war, "the whole earth is the sepulchre of illustrious men."

The Gettysburg Address

All time, he might have added, is the millennium of their glory . . . . Wheresoever throughout the civilized world the accounts of this great war are read, and down to the last period of recorded time, there will be no brighter page than that which relates the Battle of Gettysburg.

A glee club sings an ode composed for the dedication. An official rises and says: "The President of the United States."

And Lincoln, putting on his steel-bowed glasses, taking a paper out of his pocket, steps to the front of the platform, to utter the immortal words that all the world knows simply as "The Gettysburg Address":

★

Four score and seven years ago our fathers brought forth on this continent a new nation, conceived in Liberty, and dedicated to the proposition that all men are created equal.

Now we are engaged in a great civil war, testing whether that nation, or any nation so conceived and so dedicated, can long endure. We are met on a great battlefield of that war. We have come to dedicate a portion of that field, as a final resting place for those who here gave their lives that that nation might live. It is altogether fitting and proper that we should do this.

But, in a larger sense, we cannot dedicate — we cannot consecrate — we cannot hallow — this ground. The brave men, living and dead, who struggled here, have consecrated it, far above our poor power to add or detract. The world will little note, nor long remember what we say here, but it can never forget what they did here. It is for us the living, rather, to be dedicated here to the unfinished work which they who fought here have thus far so nobly advanced. It is rather for us to be here dedicated to the great task remaining for us — that from these honored dead we take increased devotion to that cause for which they gave the last full measure of devotion — that we here highly resolve that these dead shall not have died in vain — that this nation, under God, shall have a new birth of freedom — and that government of the people, by the people, for the people, shall not perish from the earth.

These few words of Abraham Lincoln are so soon over that the photographer, with his clumsy camera, has not had time to take the President's picture. The audience has hardly had time to settle itself before the speaker sat down again. Lincoln wishes he had been able to prepare a better speech. But a few persons present knew from the first that his words belonged to the ages. And those words have gone on growing in the hearts of men. They are no longer about Gettysburg alone. They are about all men everywhere who have fought for great causes and given their lives.

They are about the living everywhere who mourn and cherish the dead who have not died in vain. They are about all the inhabitants of the earth, which is the sepulchre of illustrious men. They are about the new birth of freedom for which men have lately died, and which the living are resolved must not — cannot — shall not perish.

★ 6 ★

Lincoln and Wilson

HERE are tributes to a single great American —
Abraham Lincoln. One of these was paid him
in September 1916 by another President,
Woodrow Wilson, and his noble words do honor both to
Lincoln and to the undying spirit of democracy.

Besides parts of Woodrow Wilson's address, here are also
three poems: one on Nancy Hanks, Lincoln's mother, by
Rosemary Benét; one on Anne Rutledge, by Edgar Lee
Masters; and part of one on Lincoln himself, by Edwin
Markham.

The place where a man was born reminds us first
Of homely human things that were his lot,
Before his worth and the fall of circumstance
Made him what he was — for good or ill.
The American Scripture you will hear this day
Takes us to such a spot, a rise in ground
Beside the Nolin River, Sinking Spring Farm,
Near Hodgenville, Kentucky, on a day
Sun-soaked yet soft with mid-September mist.
Here granite columns from New England's hills
And walls of marble, brought from Tennessee,
Protect a treasure valued beyond price,
A cabin built of logs and chinked with clay.
Let fancy float you there just now to stand

STATESMEN

With up-raised face beside Kentucky folk
And hear the strong, sure voice of Woodrow Wilson
Speaking as President of the United States:

*

. . . . How eloquent this little house within this shrine is of
the vigor of democracy! There is nowhere in the land any
home so remote, so humble, that it may not contain the power
of mind and heart and conscience to which nations yield and
history submits its processes . . . . This little hut was the cradle
of one of the great sons of men, a man of singular, delightful,
vital genius who presently emerged upon the great stage of
the nation's history, gaunt, shy, ungainly, but dominant and
majestic, a natural leader of men. . . . No man can explain
this, but every man can see how it demonstrates the vigor of
democracy, where every door is open, in every hamlet and
countryside, in city and wilderness alike, for the ruler to
emerge when he will and claim his leadership in the free
life. . . . .

Standing beside it, Mr. President,
"This little hut was the cradle," so you said,
And now it seems your voice grows thin and fades —
Is lost in the misty stillness of the day,
As from behind a column steps a girl
To tell us words that will some time be said
About a girl whose name was Nancy Hanks,
The mother of a boy whose name you know:

Lincoln and Wilson

If Nancy Hanks
Came back as a ghost,
Seeking news
Of what she loved most
She'd ask first
Where's my son?
What's happened to Abe?
What's he done?

Poor little Abe
Left all alone,
Except for Tom
Who's a rolling stone;
He was only nine
The year I died.
I remember still
How hard he cried.

Scraping along
In a little shack,
With hardly a shirt
To cover his back,
And a prairie wind
To blow him down,
Or pinching times
If he went to town.

You wouldn't know
About my son?
Did he grow tall?
Did he have fun?
Did he learn to read:
Did he get to town?

STATESMEN

Do you know his name?
Did he get on?

And now the voice of President Wilson
Comes back, and the sight of the listening crowd as well,
Their faces are intent, moveless in sunlight;
Their eyes are fixed, their brows are knit in thought
As Woodrow Wilson speaks:

★

.... Whatever the vigor and vitality of the stock from which
he sprang, its mere vigor and soundness do not explain where
this man got his great heart that seemed to comprehend all
mankind .... in its catholic and benignant sympathy, the
mind that sat enthroned behind those brooding, melancholy
eyes, whose vision swept many an horizon which those about
him dreamed not of, that mind that comprehended what it
had never seen, ... or that nature which seemed in its
varied richness to be the familiar of men of every way of life.
This is the sacred mystery of democracy, that its richest fruits
spring up out of soils which no man has prepared and in
circumstances amidst which they are the least expected. This
is a place alike of mystery and of reassurance ....

Again the clear voice fails upon our ears.
Its notes recede and sudden silence falls,
And someone else has stepped into our fantasy,

Lincoln and Wilson

A neighbor, this time, from not far away —
He lives beside Spoon River, is a friend
Of all those here, bears witness as he can,
To where this man's great comprehending heart
Found happiness and solace long ago.
This friend has written of her whom all can name —
Abe Lincoln's girl — you know — the one that died!
Edgar Lee Masters brings her back to us;
She lifts her voice in his immortal words:

★

Out of me unworthy and unknown,
The vibrations of deathless music:
"With malice toward none, with charity for all."
Out of me the forgiveness of millions toward millions,
And the beneficent face of a nation
Shining with justice and truth.
I am Anne Rutledge who sleep beneath these weeds,
Beloved in life of Abraham Lincoln,
Wedded to him not through union,
But through separation.
Bloom forever, O Republic,
From the dust of my bosom!

You will forgive us, Mr. President!
These interruptions are but shreds of dream
That hang about your shining sentences.
Go on — our thoughts were somehow turned aside,
But not for long, by words you said.

STATESMEN

Words that stirred us to imaginings
Speak on, Mr. President.

★

Here Lincoln had his beginnings. Here the end and consummation of that great life seem remote and a bit incredible.
And yet there was no break anywhere between beginning and end.
Nothing really incredible happened. Lincoln was unaffectedly as much at home in the White House as he was here. The test of every American must always be not where he is but *what* he is.

Not where he is but what he is, you said,
And what was he whom we have come to praise?
A thousand voices rise in glad reply.
Let this one speak, this man from Oregon,
Let all the great West answer in his words:

★

The color of the ground was in him, the red earth;
The smell and smack of elemental things:
The rectitude and patience of the cliff,
The good-will of the rain that loves all leaves;
The friendly welcome of the wayside well,
The courage of the bird that dares the sea,
The gladness of the wind that shakes the corn,
The mercy of the snow that hides all scars,

Lincoln and Wilson

The secrecy of streams that make their way
Beneath the mountain to the rifted rock;
The tolerance and equity of light
That gives as freely to the shrinking flower
As to the great oak flaring to the wind —
To the grave's low hill as to the Matterhorn
That shoulders out of the sky.
Sprung from the West,
He drank the valorous youth of a new world.
The strength of virgin forests braced his mind,
The hush of spacious prairies stilled his soul.
His words were oaks in acorns; and his thoughts
Were roots that firmly gript the granite truth.
                      .... He held his place —
Held the long purpose like a growing tree —
Held on through blame and faltered not at praise.
Towering in calm rough-hewn sublimity.
And when he fell in whirlwind, he went down
As when a lordly cedar, green with boughs,
Goes down with a great shout upon the hills,
And leaves a lonesome place against the sky.

Noon in Kentucky, hot September noon.
Now coats come off and starched white shirts are showing
Beneath the brown, lined faces of the crowd.
The President is coming to the end,
And soon the dreams that hang about his words —
Visions that other men have seen and written —
Will fade in mists of that dim yesterday
At Sinking Spring Farm beside the Nolin River.

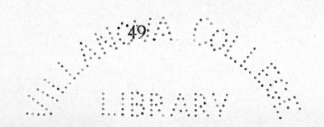

STATESMEN

I have come here today, not to utter a eulogy on Lincoln — he stands in need of none — but to endeavor to interpret the meaning of this gift to the Nation of the place of his birth and origin. The hopes of mankind cannot be kept alive by words merely, by constitutions and doctrines of right and codes of liberty. The object of democracy is to transmute these into the life and action of society, the self-denial and self-sacrifice of heroic men and women willing to make their lives an embodiment of right and service and enlightened purpose. The commands of democracy are as imperative as its privileges and opportunities are wide and generous. Its compulsion is upon us. It will be great and lift a great light for the guidance of the nations, only if we are great and carry that light high for the guidance of our own feet.

We are not worthy to stand here unless we ourselves be in deed and in truth real democrats and servants of mankind, ready to give our very lives for the freedom and justice and spiritual exaltation of the great nation which shelters and nurtures us.

Lincoln and Whitman

O F ALL great Americans, Lincoln has been the one most honored by American poets. And he is the only President with whom a great poet is associated in all our memories. That poet, of course, was Walt Whitman. Whitman lived in Washington while Lincoln was president and often saw him, though the two men seem never to have met. But while Lincoln was alive Whitman deeply felt the grandeur of his hero, and when Lincoln died he was the first to honor him in deathless words. Let us remember a time when Whitman once saw Lincoln; and then the time when the Lincoln funeral train was bearing the dead president home, and the living poet perpetuated the occasion in great verse.

Let one sound echo in our ears this hour.
Let it drift along time's lonely highway
Into our hearing, soft at first, then loud —
The rhythmic clopping of a horse's hooves.
Let it be magic sound to carry us
Somehow across the years to Washington,
Already hot with summer morning sun,
And set us down on Vermont Avenue
Near L Street — in August, 1863.

STATESMEN

Someone is listening with us here. He stands
Gazing toward the sound with such a look
As men may have but rarely in their lives,
When revelations come, as in a dream,
Of things yet unexplained. A huge fellow,
Wearing a broad, light-colored hat, blue coat;
A shirt with a frilly collar, flowing tie,
Part-hidden by his mighty, flowing beard.
He stands erect and solemn. A time has come
That must be met. He sees and we see too,
A gray horse trotting slowly and a rider
Whose face we know. As we look upon it,
A smile begins to break, first from the eyes,
Then from the lips. The man beside us bows
And lifts his hat, and though his face is young,
The hair upon his head is gleaming white.
He turns and walks away then, swiftly.
His rolling step bears his great body on
As if it were a ship that dares the trough
Of windy seas. The sound of hooves is gone
The horse and rider fade upon the sight.
Already in his room, the third-floor back,
Our tall companion writes what he has seen:

★

I saw him this morning about eight-thirty riding on Vermont
Avenue, near L Street. Mr. Lincoln on the saddle generally
rides a good-sized, easy-going gray horse, is dressed in plain
black, somewhat rusty and dusty, wears a stiff black hat and
looks about as ordinary in attire as the commonest man. I see
very plainly Abraham Lincoln's dark-brown face, with the

52

deep-cut lines, the eyes always to me with a deep latent sadness in the expression.

This look, though abstracted, happened to be directed
steadily in my eye. He bowed and smiled, but far beneath
his smile I noticed well the expression I have alluded to.
None of the artists or pictures has caught the deep, though
subtle and indirect expression, of this man's face. There is
something else there. One of the great portrait painters two
or three centuries ago is needed.

This was the fearless leader Walt had dreamed,
Come from the throbbing heart of America
To break the prison-chain the past had forged;
The manacles of custom, locks of habit
That held his country from her destiny;
A man of the people whom the people loved,
Who bore democracy a love as great
As that which Walt himself bore in his heart.
Lincoln and Whitman, immortals of our land,
Bowed to each other on the city street,
But never talked together, never knew
How the great bonds that sternly held them both
To mankind's service, might have made them friends.
But when the awful years of war were done
And martyred Lincoln lay in moveless death,
Walt felt the closeness never realized,
And driven by greater grief than he had known,
Wrote words that said for all the weeping land
What sadness filled the hearts of America:

STATESMEN

*

O Captain! my Captain! our fearful trip is done,
The ship has weather'd every rack, the prize we sought
        is won.
The port is near, the bells I hear, the people all exulting,
While follow eyes the steady keel, the vessel grim and
        daring;
          But O heart! heart! heart!
          O the bleeding drops of red,
          Where on the deck my Captain lies,
          Fallen cold and dead.

O Captain! my Captain! rise up and hear the bells;
Rise up — for you the flag is flung — for you the bugle trills,
For you bouquets and ribbon'd wreaths — for you the shores
        a-crowding,
For you they call, the swaying mass, their eager faces turning;
          Here Captain! dear father!
          This arm beneath your head!
          It is some dream that on the deck,
          You've fallen cold and dead.

My Captain does not answer, his lips are pale and still,
My father does not feel my arm, he has no pulse nor will,
The ship is anchor'd safe and sound, its voyage closed and
        done,
From fearful trip the victor ship comes in with object won;
          Exult, O shores, and ring, O bells!
          But I with mournful tread
          Walk the deck my Captain lies,
          Fallen cold and dead.

Lincoln and Whitman

And when the great dead went back home to rest,
Rolling across the land he loved — and saved,
Walt wrote a song of sorrow and of hope —
"The most sonorous anthem ever chanted
In the church of the world" — so poet Swinburne said —
For England grieved — and all throughout the earth
Who loved their fellows — and our stricken South
Who lost her warmest friend in the evil hour
When the assassin's bullet found its mark.
Now, good gray poet read to us once more
Read us this song of our democracy,
For in this elegy for him who died,
You wove both grief and triumph over death
By one whose love of mankind was so great
We feel it yet and warm our lives with it.
Read it, Walt Whitman — tell us how our land
Paid tribute to a man who lived and died
That our great people, born of many bloods —
Our union might not perish from the earth:

*

When lilacs last in the dooryard bloom'd
And the great star early droop'd in the western sky in the
        night,
I mourn'd, and yet shall mourn with ever-returning
        spring. . . .
In the dooryard fronting an old farm house near the white-
        wash'd palings,
Stands the lilac-bush tall-growing with heart-shaped leaves
        of rich green,
With many a pointed blossom rising delicate, with the per-
        fume strong I love,

55

STATESMEN

With every leaf a miracle — and from this bush in the
    dooryard,
With delicate-color'd blossoms and heart-shaped leaves of
    rich green,
A sprig with its flower I break. . . .

Over the breast of the spring, the land, amid cities,
Amid lanes and through old woods, where lately the violets
    peep'd from the ground, spotting the gray debris,
Amid the grass in the fields each side of the lanes, passing
    the endless grass,
Passing the yellow-spear'd wheat, every grain from its shroud
    in the dark-brown fields uprisen,
Passing the apple-tree blows of white and pink in the orchards,
Carrying a corpse to where it shall rest in the grave,
Night and day journeys a coffin.

Coffin that passes through lanes and streets,
Through day and night with the great cloud darkening the
    land,
With the pomp of the inloop'd flags, with the cities draped
    in black,
With the show of the States themselves as of crape-veil'd
    women standing,
With processions long and winding and the flambeaus of the
    night,
With the countless torches lit, with the silent sea of faces and
    the unbared heads
With the waiting depot, the arriving coffin, and the somber
    faces,
With dirges through the night, with the thousand voices ris-
    ing strong and solemn,
With all the mournful voices of the dirges pour'd around
    the coffin,

Lincoln and Whitman

The dim-lit churches and the shuddering organs — where
       amid these you journey,
With the tolling tolling bells' perpetual clang,
Here, coffin that slowly passes,
I give you my sprig of lilac. . . .

HOLIDAYS

★ 8 ★

Declaration of Independence

O N ANY Fourth of July in the United States, one
of our American Scriptures has the right to be
heard above all others. And on any such Fourth,
while the great words of the Declaration of Independence
ring like bells through the states, from ocean to ocean, let
us remember the first Fourth of July, in 1776. On that day
those words were still a secret behind the closed doors of
the Continental Congress in Philadelphia.

Behind those doors, on that first Fourth, the Declaration
had not sprung full-born into history. It had come out of
long and bitter debate, among real men who could not know
what the outcome of their bold resolve would be. If the cause
of independence should triumph, they would be heroes to the
new country; if it failed, they would be traitors to the old.
When they pledged their lives, their fortunes, and their
sacred honor to the support of the Declaration, they meant
each word. Their lives might be forfeited, their property
might be confiscated, and their names might be dishonored
—forever.

In the body of the Declaration on which they had at last
agreed, they set forth, with dramatic force, the grievances
driving them to their present act. But in the preamble they
rose above temporary arguments to a general assertion of the

rights of men to be free and to govern themselves. Here they took their stand with all free men, before and after.

★

When, in the Course of human events, it becomes necessary for one people to dissolve the political bands which have connected them with another, and to assume among the powers of the earth, the separate and equal station to which the Laws of Nature and of Nature's God entitle them, a decent respect to the opinions of mankind requires that they should declare the causes which impel them to the separation — We hold these truths to be self-evident, that all men are created equal, that they are endowed by their Creator with certain unalienable Rights, that among these are Life, Liberty and the pursuit of Happiness — That to secure these rights, Governments are instituted among Men, deriving their just powers from the consent of the governed, — That whenever any Form of Government becomes destructive of these ends, it is the Right of the People to alter or to abolish it, and to institute new Government, laying its foundation on such principles and organizing its powers in such form, as to them shall seem most likely to effect their Safety and Happiness. Prudence, indeed, will dictate that Governments long established should not be changed for light and transient causes; and accordingly all experience hath shewn that mankind are more disposed to suffer, while evils are sufferable, than to right themselves by abolishing the forms to which they are accustomed. But when a long train of abuses and usurpations, pursuing invariably the same Object evinces a design to reduce them under absolute Despotism, it is their right, it is their duty, to throw off such Government, and to provide new Guards for their future security . . . .

In these words a new nation declared itself. At the same time it announced the beginning of a new age in human history. But for Americans there is another Fourth almost as memorable as the first. It came fifty years later.

On the morning of the Fourth in 1826 three signers of the original Declaration were still alive. One of them was Charles Carroll of Maryland, who was to outlive them all. Another was John Adams of Massachusetts, who had helped revise the famous document. The third was Thomas Jefferson of Virginia, who had written it. They had seen the triumph of their cause. Jefferson and Adams each had been president of the United States. The year 1826 marked a half century of American independence and a half century of the rights of man.

Adams and Jefferson were invited to attend a grand celebration of the Fourth at Washington. They could not know, when their invitations came, that they would both commemorate the day by dying on it, and so make it unforgettable. They knew only that they were too infirm to undertake the journey.

But Jefferson, ten days before that Fourth, wrote a letter which perfectly sums up his memory of the Declaration and his thought about its consequences for the United States and for the world. He had written the Declaration in secrecy and uncertainty. Now he could write, on his sunny hill at Monticello, about the Declaration in the full light of the honor it had brought him and his country.

Seldom, if ever, elsewhere in history has destiny accorded

Declaration of Independence

to men the high honor of being present at a nation's birth; then, fifty years later, allowed them to assess that nation's triumph. This was Jefferson's privilege:

★

I should, indeed, with peculiar delight, have met and exchanged there congratulations personally with the small band, the remnant of that host of worthies, who joined with us on that day, in the bold and doubtful election we were to make for our country, between submission or the sword; and to have enjoyed with them the consolatory fact that our fellow citizens, after half a century of experience and prosperity, continue to approve the choice we made. May it be to the world, what I believe it will be — to some parts sooner, to others later, but finally to all — the signal of arousing men to burst the chains under which ignorance and superstition had persuaded them to bind themselves, and to assume the blessings and security of self-government.

That form which we have substituted, restores the free right to the unbounded exercise of reason and freedom of opinion. All eyes are opened, or opening, to the rights of man. The general spread of the light of science has already laid open to every view the palpable truth, that the mass of mankind has not been born with saddles on their backs, nor a favored few booted and spurred, ready to ride them legitimately, by the Grace of God.

These are grounds of hope for others. For ourselves, let the annual return of this day forever refresh our recollections of these rights, and an undiminished devotion to them.

All eyes are opened, or opening, to the rights of man.

— THOMAS JEFFERSON

PLATE NINE

THE WHITE HOUSE AT THE TIME OF
THOMAS JEFFERSON

Government of the people, by the people, for the people.
— ABRAHAM LINCOLN

PLATE TEN

THE OLD HOUSE OF REPRESENTATIVES

PAINTED BY SAMUEL F. B. MORSE. FROM THE PERMANENT COLLECTION OF THE
CORCORAN GALLERY OF ART, WASHINGTON, D. C.

66

67

. . . these United States shall serve all nations who look forward with us to the day of peaceful commerce throughout the world.

PREPARATION FOR WAR TO DEFEND COMMERCE . . . BUILDING THE FRIGATE PHILADELPHIA, BEHIND SOUTHWARK, THE OLD SWEDISH CHURCH

69

*And the rockets' red glare, the bombs bursting in air, Gave
proof through the night, that our flag was still there.*

— FRANCIS SCOTT KEY

BOMBARDMENT OF FORT McHENRY . . . ON THE MORNING OF THE 13th OF SEPTEMBER, 1814

COURTESY OF THE BETTMANN ARCHIVE, NEW YORK CITY.

70

71

Now both ships were tall torches, flaring wild into the darkness, licking at the stars.

PLATE THIRTEEN

BATTLE BETWEEN THE *SERAPIS* AND THE *BON HOMME RICHARD* UNDER JOHN PAUL JONES

COURTESY OF THE BETTMANN ARCHIVE, NEW YORK CITY.

I have just begun to fight.

— JOHN PAUL JONES

PLATE FOURTEEN

CAPT. JOHN PAUL JONES SHOOTING A SAILOR WHO HAD ATTEMPTED TO STRIKE HIS COLORS IN AN ENGAGEMENT

COURTESY OF THE METROPOLITAN MUSEUM OF ART,
NEW YORK CITY.

74

Capt. PAUL JONES ſhooting a SAILOR who had attempted to ſtrike his COLOURS in an Engagement

75

I thank God my life has been spent in a land of liberty.

— ANDREW JACKSON

PLATE FIFTEEN

GEN. ANDREW JACKSON, 1817

PAINTED BY SAMUEL LOVETT WALDO. COURTESY OF
MR. AND MRS. WILLIAM A. FISHER.

76

What most charms me is that all the citizens are brethren.
— MARQUIS DE LAFAYETTE

PLATE SIXTEEN

THE MARQUIS DE LAFAYETTE

PAINTED BY SAMUEL F. B. MORSE. COURTESY OF THE
METROPOLITAN MUSEUM OF ART, NEW YORK CITY.

78

★ 9 ★

Thanksgiving

WHEN we come in any year to the season of our national Thanksgiving, it is good to remember that this has, from the first, always been the occasion, not only of thanks for what we have received, but also of hope for what we believe lies ahead of us through the winter and beyond it. At Plymouth, in that famous November of 1621, the Pilgrims had only a small harvest from the past summer — "about a peck of meal a week to a person." But there were fish in the sea, and water fowl, and wild turkeys. And so the Pilgrims gave thanks and took fresh hope.

The first national Thanksgiving was proclaimed by Abraham Lincoln in 1863, in the midst of the Civil War. Then the great President gave thanks for "the gracious gifts of the most high God who, while dealing with us in anger for our sins, hath nevertheless remembered mercy."

Always in days like these we think of them —
The brave, the steadfast and the gentle,
Embarking on their little ship, the *Mayflower*,
And daring seas whose cold and dark, deep swell
Were omens of disaster.
Always in days like these we think of them —

81

HOLIDAYS

Holding that death were better than to lose the liberty of
      the soul.
The narrow earthy walls of the grave
Were welcome rather than to suffer the imprisonment of the
      free mind.
Now more than ever do we think of them
Striking the chains that bound them to their past —
The dearness of the English farm beside the gentle river,
The thatched roofs in the soft, sweet air of England —
Forsaking these and all warm friendships, and love of
      kinfolk,
For life beyond the vast gray wall of ocean,
A life that no one could foretell — a mystery
Hid by veils that gave no glimpse of happiness beyond.
So now we stand upon the brink of great adventure,
Setting our course across the boundless sea of future days.
Now we ride out the wildest storm of history
And look beyond the mountainous waves to see new life,
A life that men have never lived before,
A life of brotherhood among the nations and the races.
Searching for guidance — and some shining lodestar of the
      past
By which we may direct ourselves — we scan man's past
      experience
And see that little ship put into harbor on Cape Cod
And hear a voice—the voice of one young English farmer —
      William Bradford:

★

Being thus arrived in a good harbor and brought safe to land,
they fell upon their knees and blessed the God of heaven
who had brought them over the vast and furious ocean and

82

Thanksgiving

delivered them from all the perils and miseries thereof, again to set their feet on the firm and stable earth, their proper element. . . . Being thus passed the vast ocean they had now no friends to welcome them, nor inns to entertain or refresh their weather-beaten bodies, no houses or much less towns to repair to, to seek for succour.

They might have stayed beside their well-worn hearths,
Have walked old lanes grown sweet with haw and barberry;
They might have seen at journey's end the lighted windows
Of hostelries that welcomed travelers of old roads.
These they gave up — and the many-chimneyed towns,
Casting black shadows underneath an English moon,
And well-plowed fields, each furrow filled with sunlight
As dawn broke on the slopes of English hills.
Gave up for what? What drove them on their way?
Only the knowledge that no man may live
At peace with his good neighbors and himself
If other men, assuming power, shall try
To mould his thoughts to patterns not his own.
These men would worship God in their own ways.
Denied the right, they dared uncharted seas,
Seeking a new free world — no matter what the cost —
Risking the wild and frothing surf on hidden rocks,
The fury of wild animals and of wilder men.
Let William Bradford speak again of them:

*

It is recorded in scripture as a mercy to the apostle and his shipwrecked company, that the barbarians showed them no small kindness in refreshing them; but these savage barbarians, when they met with them . . . . were readier to fill their sides full of arrows than otherwise. And for the season, it was winter, and they that know the winters of that country know them to be sharp and violent and subject to cruel and fierce storms, dangerous to travel to known places, much more to search an unknown coast. Besides what could they see but a hideous and desolate wilderness, full of wild beasts and wild men? And what multitude there might be of them they knew not . . . . For summer being done, all things stand upon them with a weather-beaten face, and the whole country full of woods and thickets, represented a wild and savage hue. If they looked behind them, there was the mighty ocean which they had passed, and now as a main bar and gulf to separate them from all civil parts of the world.

Yet this was a life they welcomed with Thanksgiving,
Though it might bring cold death in many ways.
Before the spring would blossom in the woodlands
A half of them would sleep the eternal sleep.
Yet they were brave and built their houses,
Shared their food and waited through the winter
The sweet first flowering of arbutus.
And William Bradford spoke for all the Pilgrims.

★

What could now sustain them but the spirit of God and His Grace? May not and ought not the children of these fathers rightly say:

"Our Fathers were Englishmen which came over this great

ocean, and were ready to perish in this wilderness; but they
cried unto the Lord and he heard their voice and looked on
their adversity. Let them therefore praise the Lord because
He is good and His mercies endure forever. Yes, let them
which have been redeemed of the Lord show how He hath
delivered them from the hand of the oppressor. When they
wandered in the desert wilderness out of the way and found
no city to dwell in, both hungry and thirsty — their soul was
overwhelmed in them. Let them confess before the Lord
His loving kindness and His wonderful works before the
sons of men."

We are the children of these fathers.
We are the children of all the old nations,
Bound together by all that is good in many heritages.
We still fight the good fight for all mankind.
And with God's aid we have delivered men from the hand
        of the oppressor.
But winning to the shores of peace is not enough.
There stands the forest of the future.
The new life we shall face will not return us to old ways,
There is no going back — but we are glad.
We turn our faces to the sunlight of new dawns
And like those men of long ago,
The brave, the steadfast, and the gentle,
Embarking on their little ship, the *Mayflower*,
We praise the Lord for troubles He has brought us through.
We praise Him for His matching us against the challenge
        of this hour.
To Him, upon the threshold of new life, we raise
Our hymn of deep Thanksgiving.

10

The First Memorial Day

MEMORIAL DAY in the United States began with a little local spontaneous ceremony that spread over the nation like the healing new grass over a battlefield.

In the spring of 1866 three good and gentle ladies of Columbus, Mississippi, on the Tombigbee River, went often to Friendship Cemetery in the town to tend the graves of soldiers who had died in the Columbus Military Hospital in the early years of the war. The example these three set — Miss Moreton, and Mrs. Fontaine, and Mrs. Hill — led others to join them in a public memorial on April 25th.

A long procession made its way to the cemetery. First came the young girls, all in white. Then, in black, the women who were married, or who had lost their husbands. And then in carriages came the aged . . . and everyone who went carried a bouquet, or a chaplet of spring blossoms. They halted by the graves and formed a square, and they heard a prayer and an address, and then they laid their flowers as badges of honor upon their dead.

Some fourteen hundred Confederate dead lay there, and somewhat apart from them were the graves of about forty Northern soldiers who had died in Columbus as prisoners of war. And now the women of Columbus, Mississippi, with a single impulse, seem to have said in their hearts: "But after all, these other soldiers were the sons and the brothers and the husbands of women. In the fraternity of death there can be no division." And they laid flowers on the Yankee graves as well.

The news spread everywhere. In Ithaca, New York, a lawyer named Francis Miles Finch heard the story. He wrote a poem, and the next year the *Atlantic Monthly* printed it, and it was reprinted in the newspapers and memorized and debated. Steadily and surely the generous example of the women of Columbus, and Finch's eloquence, mounted and prevailed over the bitterness of conflict.

The poem has been recited on scores of Memorial Days since then, in thousands of American towns and villages — generally by earnest little girls in starched dresses. Here are the words that Francis Miles Finch wrote when he heard of the tribute of the gallant women to all the Americans who lay asleep, side by side, in the graveyard called Friendship, in Columbus:

*

THE BLUE AND THE GRAY

By the flow of the inland river,
Whence the fleets of iron have fled,
Where the blades of the grave grass quiver,
Asleep are the ranks of the dead; —

HOLIDAYS

Under the sod and the dew,
Waiting the judgment day; —
Under the one, the Blue;
Under the other, the Gray.

These in the robings of glory,
Those in the gloom of defeat,
All with the battle blood gory,
In the dusk of eternity meet; —
Under the sod and the dew,
Waiting the judgment day; —
Under the laurel, the Blue;
Under the willow, the Gray.

From the silence of sorrowful hours
The desolate mourners go,
Lovingly laden with flowers
Alike for the friend and the foe; —
Under the sod and the dew,
Waiting the judgment day; —
Under the roses, the Blue;
Under the lilies, the Gray.

So with an equal splendor
The morning sunrays fall,
With a touch, impartially tender,
On the blossoms blooming for all; —
Under the sod and the dew,
Waiting the judgment day; —
'Broidered with gold, the Blue;
Mellowed with gold, the Gray.
So, when the summer calleth,
On forest and field of grain

The First Memorial Day

With an equal murmur falleth
The cooling drip of the rain; —
Under the sod and the dew,
Waiting the judgment day; —
Wet with the rain, the Blue;
Wet with the rain, the Gray.

Sadly, but not with upbraiding,
The generous deed was done;
In the storm of the years that are fading,
No braver battle was won; —
Under the sod and the dew,
Waiting the judgment day; —
Under the blossoms, the Blue;
Under the garlands, the Gray.

No more shall the war-cry sever,
Or the winding rivers be red;
They banish our anger forever
When they laurel the graves of our dead; —
Under the sod and the dew,
Waiting the judgment day; —
Love and tears for the Blue,
Tears and love for the Gray.

11

Aviation Day

DECEMBER 17 is Aviation Day. That date was so designated because it was on December 17, 1903, that the Wright brothers made their first hesitant brief flight at Kitty Hawk. There were only five spectators on the lonely North Carolina beach when they got their clumsy machine into the air, and the newspapers barely mentioned the great achievement.

Today men use the skies as readily as their fathers used the sea. Human flight has become a part of human life — in peace and in war. In war the armored eagles developed from that fragile machine which the Wrights flew at Kitty Hawk four decades ago are war's most deadly weapons.

This air-war fulfills a prophecy made by a great American long ago. In 1783, Benjamin Franklin witnessed in Paris the earliest flights of men in balloons. Here is what he wrote a friend about man's discovery of a means to soar into the skies:

★

It . . . . may possibly give a new turn to human affairs. Convincing sovereigns of the folly of wars may perhaps be one effect of it, since it will be impracticable for the most potent of them to guard his dominions. Five thousand balloons, capable of raising two men each, could not cost more than two ships of the line; and where is the prince who can afford so to cover his country with troops for its defence as that ten thousand men descending from the clouds might not in many places do an infinite deal of mischief before a force could be brought together to repel them? . . . .

Of course, Franklin was thinking of balloons, not of airplanes, and of parachute troops, not of bombs, but he foresaw the first principles of future air-war.

It took a long time for men to go beyond balloons, that would rise into the air like bubbles, to planes that would take off and fly like birds. But the day came when that experiment was made successfully by two young Americans, Orville and Wilbur Wright.

What happened that December 17, 1903, on the beach at Kitty Hawk in North Carolina, is one of the most important chapters of our American Scriptures. Even today, we are only beginning to realize how far-reaching the achievement of the Wright brothers was in its effect upon our lives, and upon the whole way of living in the world that we are making for the future.

In "The Campers at Kitty Hawk," John Dos Passos tells the story unforgettably:

★

On December seventeenth, nineteen hundred and three, Bishop Wright of the United Brethren onetime editor of the *Religious Telescope* received in his frame house on Hawthorn Street in Dayton, Ohio, a telegram from his boys Wilbur and Orville who'd gotten it into their heads to spend their vacations in a little camp out on the dunes of the North Carolina coast tinkering with a homemade glider they'd knocked together themselves. The telegram read:

SUCCESS FOUR FLIGHTS THURSDAY MORNING
ALL AGAINST TWENTYONE MILE WIND
STARTED FROM LEVEL WITH ENGINEPOWER
ALONE AVERAGE SPEED THROUGH AIR
THIRTYONE MILES LONGEST FIFTYSEVEN
SECONDS INFORM PRESS HOME CHRISTMAS

The figures were a little wrong because the telegraph operator misread Orville's hasty penciled scrawl
but the fact remains
that a couple of young bicycle mechanics from Dayton, Ohio
had designed, constructed and flown
for the first time ever a practical airplane.

After running the motor a few minutes to heat it up I released the wire that held the machine to the track and the machine started forward into the wind. Wilbur ran at the side of the machine holding the wing to balance it on the track. Unlike the start on the 14th made in a calm the machine facing a 27 mile wind started very slowly. . . . Wilbur was able to stay with it until it lifted from the track after a forty-foot run. One of the lifesaving men snapped the camera for us taking a picture just as it reached the end of the track and the machine had risen to a height of about two feet. . . . The course of the flight up and down was extremely erratic, partly due to the irregularities of the air, partly to lack of experience in handling this machine. A sudden dart when a little over a hundred and twenty feet from the point at which it rose in the air ended the flight. . . . This flight lasted only 12 seconds but it was nevertheless the first in the history of the world in which a machine carrying a man had raised itself by its own power into the air in full flight, had sailed forward without reduction of speed and had finally landed at a point as high as that from which it started.

A little later in the day the machine was caught in a gust of wind and turned over and smashed, almost killing the coastguardsman who tried to hold it down;
   it was too bad
   but the Wright brothers were too happy to care
   they'd proved that the damn thing flew.

When these points had been definitely established we at once packed our goods and returned home knowing that the age of the flying machine had come at last.

They were home for Christmas in Dayton, Ohio, where they'd been born in the seventies of a family who had been settled west of the Alleghenies since eighteen fourteen, in Dayton, Ohio, where they'd been to grammarschool and high-school and joined their father's church and played baseball and hockey and worked out on the parallel bars and the flying swing and sold newspapers and built themselves a printing-press out of odds and ends from the junkheap and flown kites and tinkered with mechanical contraptions and gone around town as boys doing odd jobs to turn an honest penny.

The folks claimed it was the bishop's bringing home a helicopter, a fiftycent mechanical toy made of two fans worked by elastic bands that was supposed to hover in the air, that had got his two youngest boys hipped on the subject of flight

93

so that they stayed home instead of marrying the way the others boys did, and puttered all day about the house picking up a living with jobprinting,

bicyclerepair work,

sitting up late nights reading books on aerodynamics.

Still they were sincere churchmembers, their bicycle business was prosperous, a man could rely on their word. They were popular in Dayton.

In those days flyingmachines were the big laugh of all the crackerbarrel philosophers. Langley's and Chanute's unsuccessful experiments had been jeered down with an I-told-you-so that rang from coast to coast. The Wright's big problem was to find a place secluded enough to carry on their experiments without being the horselaugh of the countryside. Then they had no money to spend;

they were practical mechanics; when they needed anything they built it themselves.

They hit on Kitty Hawk,

on the great sand dunes and sandy banks that stretch south towards Hatteras seaward of Albemarle Sound,

a vast stretch of seabeach

empty except for a coastguard station, a few fishermen's shacks and the swarms of mosquitoes and the ticks and chiggers in the crabgrass behind the dunes

and overhead the gulls and swooping terns, in the evening fishhawks and cranes flapping across the salt-marshes, occasionally eagles

that the Wright brothers followed soaring with their eyes

as Leonardo watched them centuries before

straining his sharp eyes to apprehend

the laws of flight.

Aviation Day

Four miles across the loose sand from the scattering of shacks, the Wright brothers built themselves a camp and a shed for their gliders. It was a long way to pack their groceries, their tools, anything they happened to need; in summer it was hot as blazes, the mosquitoes were hell;

but they were alone there

and they'd figured out that the loose sand was as soft as anything they could find to fall in.

There with a glider made of two planes and a tail in which they lay flat on their bellies and controlled the warp of the planes by shimmying their hips, taking off again and again all day from a big dune named Kill Devil Hill,

they learned to fly.

Once they'd managed to hover for a few seconds
and soar ever so slightly on a rising aircurrent
they decided the time had come
to put a motor in their biplane.

Back in the shop in Dayton, Ohio, they built an airtunnel, which is their first great contribution to the science of flying, and tried out model planes in it.

They couldn't interest any builders of gasoline engines so they had to build their own motor.

It worked; after that Christmas of nineteen three the Wright brothers weren't doing it for fun any more; they gave up their bicycle business, got the use of a big old cowpasture belonging to the local banker for practice flights, spent all the time when they weren't working on their machine in promotion, worrying about patents, infringements, spies, trying to interest government officials, to make sense out of the smooth involved heartbreaking remarks of lawyers.

In two years they had a plane that would cover twenty-four miles at a stretch round and round the cowpasture.

HOLIDAYS

People on the interurban car used to crane their necks out
of the windows when they passed along the edge of the field,
startled by the clattering pop pop of the old Wright motor
and the sight of the white biplane like a pair of ironingboards
one on top of the other chugging along a good fifty feet in
the air. The cows soon got used to it.

As the flights got longer
the Wright brothers got backers,
engaged in lawsuits,
lay in their beds at night sleepless with the whine of phantom millions, worse than the mosquitoes at Kitty Hawk.

In nineteen seven they went to Paris,
allowed themselves to be togged out in dress suits and
silk hats,
learned to tip waiters
talked with governmment experts, got used to gold braid
and postponements and vandyke beards and the outspread
palms of politicos. For amusement
they played diabolo in the Tuileries gardens.

They gave publicized flights at Fort Myers, where they
had their first fatal crackup, St. Petersburg, Paris, Berlin;
at Pau they were all the rage,
such an attraction that the hotelkeeper
wouldn't charge them for their room.
Alfonso of Spain shook hands with them and was photographed sitting in the machine,
King Edward watched a flight,
the Crown Prince insisted on being taken up,
the rain of medals began.

They were congratulated by the Czar

Aviation Day

and the King of Italy and the amateurs of sport, and the society climbers and the papal titles,
and decorated by a society for universal peace.

Aeronautics became the sport of the day.
The Wrights don't seem to have been very much impressed by the upholstery and the braid and the gold medals and the parades of plush horses,
they remained practical mechanics
and insisted on doing all their own work themselves,
even to filling the gasolinetank.

In nineteen eleven they were back on the dunes
at Kitty Hawk with a new glider.
Orville stayed up in the air for nine and a half minutes,
which remained a long time the record for motorless flight.
The same year Wilbur died of typhoidfever in Dayton.
In the rush of new names: Farman, Bleriot, Curtiss, Ferber, Esnault-Peltrie, Delagrange;
in the snorting impact of bombs and the whine and rattle of shrapnel and the sudden stutter of machineguns after the motor's been shut off overhead,
and we flatten into the mud
and make ourselves small cowering in the corners of ruined walls,
the Wright brothers passed out of the headlines
but not even headlines or the bitter smear of newsprint or the choke of smokescreen and gas or chatter of brokers on the stockmarket or barking of phantom millions or oratory of brasshats laying wreaths on new monuments
can blur the memory
of the chilly December day
two shivering bicycle mechanics from Dayton, Ohio,
first felt their homemade contraption

HOLIDAYS

whittled out of hickory sticks,
gummed together with Arnstein's bicycle cement,
stretched with muslin they'd sewn on their sister's sewing-machine in their own backyard on Hawthorn Street in Dayton, Ohio,
soar into the air
above the dunes and the wide beach
at Kitty Hawk.

★ 12 ★

Flag Day

Oₙₑ famous and favorite American Scripture was written by an American whose name remains publicly a secret, though many people probably know it. What he here wrote first appeared as an editorial in *The New York Times*. It was meant to speak for the newspaper as well as for the individual writer. But his salute to "Flag Day — 1940" has been accepted by countless Americans as speaking for them too.

In Americans who love their country best there is always a double love — for the community or section in which they live and know best, and for the country as a whole, which they are proud to belong to.

When you read the anonymous "Flag Day — 1940", you feel that you are walking affectionately through the part of America that you know at first-hand, and yet, at the same time, magnificently soaring over the whole America from ocean to ocean.

★

What is a flag? What's the love of country for which it stands? Maybe it begins with the love of the land itself. It is the fog rolling in with the tide at Eastport, or through the Golden Gate and among the towers of San Francisco. It is the sun coming up behind the White Mountains, over the Green, throwing a shining glory on Lake Champlain and above the Adirondacks. It is the storied Mississippi, rolling swift and muddy past St. Louis, rolling past Cairo, pouring down past the levees of New Orleans. It is lazy noontide in the pines of Carolina, it is a sea of wheat rippling in western Kansas, it is the San Francisco peaks, far north across the glowing nakedness of Arizona, it is the Grand Canyon and a little stream coming down out of a New England ridge, in which are trout.

It is men at work. It is the storm-tossed fishermen coming into Gloucester and Providence and Astoria. It is the farmer riding his great machine in the dust of harvest, the dairyman going to the barn before sunrise, the lineman mending the broken wire, the miner drilling for the blast. It is the servants of the fire in the murky splendor of Pittsburgh, between the Allegheny and the Monongahela, the trucks rumbling through the night, the locomotive engineer bringing the train in on time, the pilot in the clouds, the riveter running along the beam a hundred feet in the air. It is the clerk in the office, the housewife doing the dishes, and sending the children off to school. It is the teacher, doctor and parson tending and helping, body and soul, for small reward.

It is small things remembered, the little corners of the land, the houses, the people that each one loves. We love our country because there was a little tree on a hill, and grass thereon, and a sweet valley below; because the hurdy-gurdy man came along on a sunny morning in a city street; because a beach or a farm or a lane or a house that might not seem so much to others, was once, for each of us, magic.

It is voices that are remembered, only no longer heard. It is parents, friends, the lazy chat of a street and store and office, and the ease of mind that makes life tranquil. It is summer and winter, rain and sun and storm. These are flesh of our flesh, bone of our bone, blood of our blood, a lasting part of what we are, each of us and all of us together.

It is stories told. It is the Pilgrims dying in their first dreadful winter. It is the minute-man standing his ground at Concord Bridge, and dying there. It is the army in rags, sick, freezing, starving at Valley Forge. It is the wagons and the men on foot going westward over Cumberland Gap, floating down the great rivers, rolling over the great plains. It is the settler hacking fiercely at the primeval forest on his new, his own lands. It is Thoreau at Walden Pond, Lincoln at Cooper Union, and Lee riding home from Appomattox. It is corruption and disgrace, answered always by men who would not let the flag lie in the dust, who have stood up in every generation to fight for the old ideals and the old rights, at risk of ruin or of life itself.

It is a great multitude of people on pilgrimage, common and ordinary people, charged with the usual human failings, yet filled with such a hope as never caught the imaginations and the hearts of any nation on earth before; the hope of liberty; the hope of justice; the hope of a land in which a man can stand straight without fear, without rancor.

The land and the people of the flag — the land of a continent, the people of every race, the flag a symbol of what humanity may aspire to when the wars are over and the barriers are down — to these each generation must be dedicated and consecrated anew, to defend with life itself, if need be, but above all, in friendliness, in hope, in courage, to live for.

To read "Flag Day — 1940," and to see that American panorama unfolding, east, west, north and south, past and present, is also to think of places elsewhere on the earth where the American flag has recently flown, because Americans were there.

Can the earth ever seem so vast to us as it used to seem? Even when all these Americans are back in America, can the places they have been to, ever seem really foreign to us? The friends our young men have made round the earth — shall we not go on thinking of them as friends and neighbors of ours on the globe we all inhabit?

HEROES

★ 13 ★

Washington at the Delaware

THE American Scriptures tell one great Christmas story. It holds no word of Yuletide warmth and cheer, of children and firelight and a glittering tree. It is a tale of hundreds of ragged, miserable men who tramped long miles through killing cold and fierce wind to do battle for human freedom. Hardship and sacrifice are the only ornaments of this story—lack-luster and grim. But there is a happy ending.

The story begins with a tall soldier at that moment of the afternoon of December 14, 1776, when he is writing a letter. Somewhere in Pennsylvania General George Washington, lonely and discouraged, bends his serious, pock-marked face above the paper that lies in front of him:

★

Before this comes to hand, you will have heard of the melancholy situation of our affairs. I do not mean now to detail our misfortunes. With a handful of men, compared to the enemy's force, we have been pushed through the Jerseys (without being able to make the smallest opposition) and to pass the Delaware. General Howe is now on the other side and beyond all question means if possible to possess himself of Philadelphia. His troops are extended from Panny Town to Burlington; the main body, from the last advices, at the former and within the neighborhood of Trenton. I wish it were in my power to tell you that appearances were much against him. At present I confess they are not . . . . A lucky blow in this quarter would most certainly raise the spirits of the people which are quite sunk by our late misfortunes.

The story continues on a wild dark hour of the eleventh day after the general wrote his letter — Christmas.

The morning had been foreboding and chill. There was too much work to celebrate holiday. At noon twenty-four hundred men were ordered out to march the twelve miles to the Delaware. Night settled soon after they reached its dark waters. Then a wind began to blow in savage gusts. Cold rain rode upon it — then rattling hail — and silent biting snow. Fires blazed, dimmed, and blazed again beside the ice-jammed river.

Among the farmers, storekeepers, blacksmiths, clerks of Washington's dwindling little army, as it retreated across New Jersey, had been an English-born corset-maker, now turned journalist — Thomas Paine. Night after night of that bleak and desperate December he had sat with a drum between his knees straining to see by the occasional flare of his campfire what he was writing on the paper that lay on the taut drumhead.

Let one flame strike through the darkness of the years just long enough for us to hear the voice of a far-off sergeant as he reads two of Tom Paine's sentences to his men — two sentences that will stand by and comfort them in the suffering and danger they are about to undergo —

★

I have as little superstittion in me as any man living; but my secret opinion has ever been and still is, that God Almighty will not give up a people to military destruction or leave them unsupportedly to perish, who have so earnestly and so repeatedly sought to avoid the calamities of war by every decent method which wisdom could invent. Neither have I so much of the infidel in me as to suppose that He has relinquished the government of the world.

It is three o'clock in the morning and the long flat-bottomed barges swing against the river shore. The ice grates and groans against their sides. Once — in the old days of peace — they carried iron-ore downriver. Sixty feet of sturdy planking eight feet wide, railed high above the floor, they are landing barges not very different from the thousands that were built in this country in the recent war. Yankee Colonel John Glover's regiment of Marblehead fishermen handle them as easily as they would Gloucester luggers.

This is not Washington Crossing the Delaware as the German painter, Leutze, imagined it in the famous picture. This is the real thing. This is Glover setting Washington and his army on the other side of the river — Glover and his Marblehead boys packing the troops in, sometimes a regiment to a boat — for the regiments are pitifully small — and poling them through three hundred yards of ice-choked water to the Jersey shore. The guns of the artillery creak aboard. The flanks of the horses are steaming. Their hooves beat a strong tattoo on the floor-boards.

On the far side at four o'clock two columns set out by different roads towards Trenton. Two men died on that march — trudging desperately, heavily on until all warmth had left their blood and they fell lifeless. But so perfectly had John Glover done his job — so surely had George

Washington at the Delaware

Washington planned this Christmas night's work — that the first shot of the first column had hardly split the dawn before it was echoed by a volley from the second. Heavy with their drinking of the night before, confused and frightened, the hired German enemies raced from their barracks and formed for battle.

A sharp voice spoke from the American ranks — "Charge bayonets!" — and the Hessians turned and ran for their lives.

It was all over in a half-hour. The German commander had been killed and a thousand of his men captured. Now there was left only the return to camp. It was a happy journey. The American drummers pounded on the new brass drums they had captured. Ragged, collarless, shoeless, the men of the line strutted in fancy brass caps surrendered by their frightened prisoners. There was a great shouting and singing. Somehow the air seemed warmer.

And 18-year-old David How of Methuen, Massachusetts, had strength enough at the end of the day to write into his diary, spelling out the words wrongly, laboriously:

★

"December 26. This morning at four o'clock we set off with our field pieces. Marched eight miles to Trenton where we were attacked by a number of Hessians and we took a thousand of them besides killed some. Then we marched back and got to the river at night and got over all the Hessians."

David How and his comrades gave to their country in those bitter hours so long ago its greatest Christmas present. Today

— we are still saying our thanks. Thanks to the two who gave their lives in that knifelike and awful wind. Thanks to Colonel John Glover, for we are remembering him and the men of Marblehead. And thanks to General Washington.

For in the darkest days of the Revolution these men proved what has been proved again and again — that men who fight for liberty will not know defeat. On the day of the birth of the Christ child they set out to defend those principles and ideals which were taught by Christ the man. Theirs was an offering not unlike his — a gift of pain and suffering, even death if it were necessary — that their children might live in peace in a free world.

The new nation rejoiced in their triumph with ringing of bells and cheering and singing of songs. We still rejoice in it and look upon it as an omen of better things. For no Christmas gift to the United States of America can be so precious as a victory in the cause of freedom.

★ 14 ★

The Bon Homme Richard

THERE IS an American aircraft carrier which bears a name as old and as honored as any name in the American Navy, the *Bon Homme Richard*. Hearing that proud name, we remember the first *Bon Homme Richard*, named after Poor Richard in honor of Benjamin Franklin, and commanded by Captain John Paul Jones. That, in turn, reminds us of the first great battle in American naval history, between John Paul Jones's *Bon Homme Richard* and the British *Serapis*.

It was fought in distant waters, off the enemy's coast. Then, in September 1779, our Navy carried the war to the enemy, as our Navy has since done, in how many seas and oceans!

And that day in September 1779 gave us the first never-forgotten words ever spoken by an American naval hero. For, at a moment when it seemed that the battle might go against us, John Paul Jones shouted his immortal defiance: "I have not yet begun to fight!"

Those words still live and burn in the American memory. Once they were John Paul Jones's words. Now, they are the words of every man in our Navy — the words of every American.

HEROES

It was in late September off Flamborough Head
That John Paul Jones, sailing the quiet dusk
In his black, lumbering East Indiaman,
The *Bon Homme Richard*, mounted with old cannon,
Beheld the yellow warship *Serapis*,
The prideful boast of all the British fleet.
Like some great moon within a deep black sky,
Shepherding fleecy clouds, she held close guard
On forty-one white sail. The moon itself
Rose from the sea, lighting the *Serapis*,
Striking quick glints of fire from her bright guns;
And the *Bon Homme Richard*, then, all canvas set,
Gave chase — and all the frightened merchantmen
Fluttered toward shore, their sails invisible
Against the high, white-shining cliffs of home.

Above those chalk walls burned the yellow lamps
Of British cottages; but all winked out
As voices calling, echoing through the night,
Summoned the safe-at-home to come and watch
A drama of the sea. Huddled they stood
Upon the headland looking down the moon-path
Where two great ships, like savage beasts of prey,
Leaped toward each other.

Come back, Nathaniel Fanning,
Midshipman, Stonington, Connecticut,
From the good Yankee heaven you inhabit,
And tell us how you fought and what you saw:

The Bon Homme Richard

*

At quarter past eight, just as the moon was rising, the weather being clear, the surface being perfectly smooth, even as a millpond, the enemy hailed us thus: "What ship is that?" The answer from our ship was: "Come a little nearer and I will tell you." The next question by the enemy in a contemptuous manner, "What are you laden with?" The answer returned was, if my recollection does not deceive me, "Round grape, and double-headed shot!" And instantly the *Serapis* poured her range of upper- and quarter-deck guns upon us. We returned the enemy's fire and thus the battle began. All this time our tops kept up an incessant and well-directed fire into the enemy's tops, which did great execution. The *Serapis* continued to take a position either under our stern or athwart our bow; gauled us in such a manner that our men fell in all parts of the ship by scores.

Accordingly, Captain Jones ordered the sailing master (a true-blooded Yankee whose name was Stacy) to lay the enemy's ship on board. As the *Serapis* soon after passed across our forefoot, our helm was put hard aweather, the main and mizzen topsails, then braced aback, were filled away, a fresh blow of wind swelling them at that instant shot our ship quick ahead and she ran her jib-boom between the enemy's starboard mizzen shrouds. Jones at the same time cried out: "Well done, my brave lads, we have got her! Now throw on board the grappling irons and stand by for boarding."

The watching crowd along the shore cried out
As lower sails of the great *Serapis*

III

May the God of the Heavens and Earth smile ... on this work ... and may he render it subservient to the best interests of the human race.

—DeWitt Clinton

THE OPENING OF THE ERIE CANAL, NOVEMBER, 1835 .... THE AMERICAN "GRAND, GALA FLEET," CIRCLING ABOUT THE BRITISH SLOOPS OF WAR *SWALLOW* AND *KINGFISHER* IN NEW YORK HARBOR

PAINTED BY ANTHONY IMBERT. COURTESY OF THE BLAND GALLERY, NEW YORK CITY.

Our goal today, as in the past, is not to serve ourselves but all mankind.

115

The progress of the United States under our free and happy institutions has surpassed the most sanguine hopes.

—ANDREW JACKSON

PLATE NINETEEN

SOUTH STREET FROM MAIDEN LANE, NEW YORK CITY

AQUATINT BY W. J. BENNETT. FROM THE PHELPS STOKES COLLECTION. COURTESY OF NEW YORK PUBLIC LIBRARY, NEW YORK CITY.

116

117

What is a flag? . . . It is the storm-tossed fishermen coming into Gloucester and Providence and Astoria.

— FLAG DAY, 1940

PLATE TWENTY

THE SPERM WHALE . . . THE CAPTURE

FROM A LITHOGRAPH BY ENDICOTT AND COMPANY. COURTESY OF THE OLD PRINT SHOP, NEW YORK CITY.

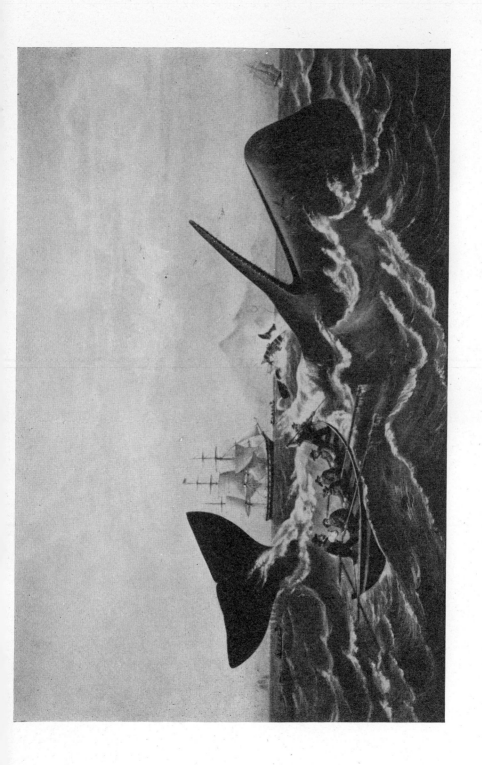

What is a flag? ... It is the clerk in the office, the housewife doing the dishes and sending the children off to school.

— FLAG DAY, 1940

PLATE TWENTY-ONE

YANKEE PEDDLER

PAINTED BY JOHN WHETTON EHNINGER, COURTESY OF THE NEWARK MUSEUM, NEWARK, NEW JERSEY.

121

What is a flag? . . . It is corruption and disgrace, answered always by men who would not let the flag lie in the dust.

— FLAG DAY, 1940

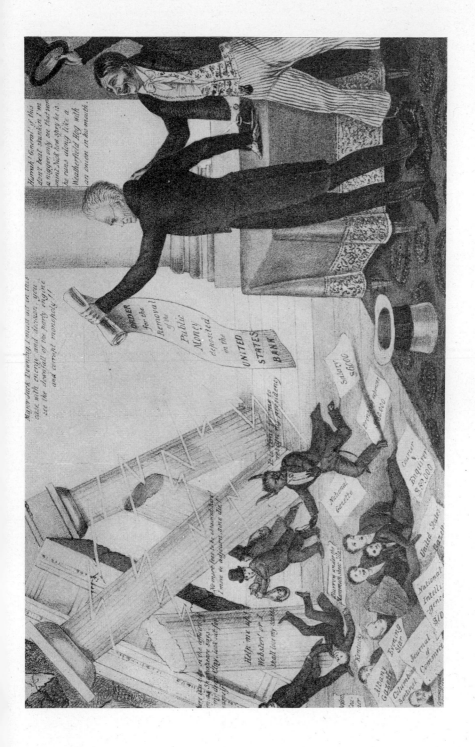

Thermopylae had her messenger of defeat. The Alamo had none.

PLATE TWENTY-THREE

THE FALL OF THE ALAMO

PAINTED BY T. GENTILY. COURTESY OF THE BETTMAN ARCHIVE, NEW YORK CITY.

124

FALL OF THE ALAMO

Where they led, we have followed.

PLATE TWENTY-FOUR

DANIEL BOONE ESCORTING A BAND OF PIONEERS INTO THE WESTERN COUNTRY

PAINTED BY GEORGE CALEB BINGHAM. COURTESY OF WASHINGTON UNIVERSITY, ST. LOUIS, MISSOURI.

126

The Bon Homme Richard

Caught fire. Flame climbed the rigging suddenly —
It crossed upon the locked yards up above
And raced back down to the American deck.
Now both ships were tall torches flaring wild
Into the darkness, licking at the stars.
The guns were silent and the only sounds
Were crackling of the blaze and men's hoarse shouts.
John Paul Jones stood by his three nine-pounders,
The only cannon of his double score
Now left to fire upon the enemy.
At their first shot two of his guns had burst
And all the others had been stilled by lead
From row on row of British thunderers.
Through jagged holes below her water line
The sea filled up the *Bon Homme Richard's* hold.
"Your ensign's gone," cried someone suddenly
From out the *Serapis*, "shot clean away,
If you have struck your colors there below
Why don't you haul your Yankee pennant down?"
"Ay! ay!", cried John Paul Jones at him, "We'll do it
When we can fight no longer." Then he yelled
Much louder: "We shall see yours come down first,
For Yankees do not haul their colors down
Till they are fairly beaten." Cannon roared
And once again the battling crews were joined,
The while the *Bon Homme Richard*, settling slow,
Lost men and guns and timbers, one by one.

Come back and tell us of your sinking ship,
Captain of our Navy's mighty fleet,
Read, Captain Jones, the words that you once wrote
To good Ben Franklin telling how you fared:

129

HEROES

*

My situation was really deplorable; the *Bon Homme Richard* received various shots under water; . . . the leak gained on the pumps; . . . there was five feet of water in the hold, the fire broke out in various parts of the ship . . . the rudder was cut entirely off, the stern-frame and transoms were almost entirely cut away . . . and timbers by the lower deck, especially from the mainmast to the stern, being greatly decayed with age, were mangled beyond my power of description . . . My treacherous master-at-arms let loose all my prisoners without my knowledge, and my prospects became gloomy indeed. I would not, however, give up the point.

And at that moment when you knew all this
A voice rose high above the din of arms —
The British captain calling out to you,
And asking of you: "Have you struck your flag?"
Say to us, John Paul Jones, the words you said
In answer, words that live as boldly now
As in that hopeless, fateful, desperate hour,
When only honor was still left to you.

*

I have not yet begun to fight!

Now from the tops a lank Nantucketer
Hurled hand-grenades down on the British deck,

The Bon Homme Richard

And one of these, thrown by his cunning hand,
Dropped down the upper hatch of the *Serapis*
And poured its fire into her store of powder.
Then tongues of searing flame ran through the ship,
And more than twenty corpses strewed the deck.
The three nine-pounders roared out once again,
And like a pine resisting a great wind,
The mighty mainmast of the *Serapis*
Trembled and groaned — but high above the sound
Men's voices fell on unbelieving ears,
Shouting: "Quarter! Quarter! Quarter!
For heaven's own sweet sake!"

The fight was won, but now the *Bon Homme Richard*
Was sinking fast. Her unharmed men in haste
Removed their wounded comrades to her prize.
Then, standing at the rail of the *Serapis*,
They watched the wind whip up the waves until,
Once more in moonlight, gallant and unafraid,
The good old ship went down, and John Paul Jones,
With such a grief as he could not express,
Had his last tear-dimmed glimpse of mast and spars,
As depths of ocean took her for their own.

But she was mother of a stout, courageous brood —
Gray ships that plowed the waters of the world,
Daring great odds in memory of her,
Gray corsairs of cold North Atlantic waves,
Strong battlers in the heat of southern seas —
And every man of all our Navy's crews
Bore in his heart the *Bon Homme Richard* story,
Remembered too, his comrades who went down
Upon the slanting decks of the *Wasp,* the *Beattie,*

HEROES

The *Helena* and the brave *Lexington*,
And other gallant warriors of the deep.
Americans, remember John Paul Jones
Alone amid the wreckage of his ship,
And saying to the foe immortal words:

★

I have not yet begun to fight!

★ 15 ★

Stonewall Jackson

EVERY year on May 10 the Carolinas celebrate their Memorial Day. And there and elsewhere many Americans remember that May 10 is the day Stonewall Jackson died in battle, at Chancellorsville in 1863.

Whether our grandfathers or great-grandfathers fought with Stonewall Jackson or against him, we all hold his memory in special honor and affection. He is for us a classic figure with a classic name — Stonewall. How many know that his name was Thomas Jonathan Jackson? How many know that he had been a professor at the Virginia Military Institute before he joined the Confederate Army? How many know, even, what actual part he played in carrying out Lee's great strategy?

These things are half-lost in the heroic legend of Stonewall Jackson as a fiery general in a weather-beaten uniform — stern, devout, and worshiped by his men. Always he said: "Push the attack." One of his officers told him the enemy was beating him back. "Then we will give them the bayonet," Jackson said. Another officer said he would not have been surprised if Jackson had ordered him to assault the North Pole. Jackson went where it seemed impossible to go, and his men followed cheering.

HEROES

Bring hyacinth, magnolia and crepe-myrtle,
Wisteria, mimosa and sweet olive,
Virginia creeper, coral vine, cape-jasmine,
And heap them on the earth that gave them life.
Then bid the mocking-bird be still a moment
The while from out the spreading fragrance lifts
The semblance of a dream once held by men:
This is the hour in which the South remembers.

Stand by the simple stone that marks his grave
And see in distant sky those blue-stained hills
That shadow Shenandoah's silver stream.
There sleeps the valley that he loved and fought for,
The loved, bold leader of Virginia's sons,
Great Stonewall Jackson, who lies here at rest.
Today the sons of those who fought against him
Bare reverent heads above these Southern flowers,
Clasp hands with sons of raiders whom he led,
And honoring him, do honor to all men
Who wore with love and pride, Confederate gray.
Here in this sun-blessed spot, God's peaceful acre,
Lie others slain beneath the stars and bars,
And on the breeze that lifts the flags above them
Come voices that were rich and strong and merry
By campfires more than eighty years ago,
Repeating words that one good comrade wrote
And all have loved and sung upon the march.
Speak, Southern soldiers, you — the gallant dead
Who fought with Stonewall by the Shenandoah:

*

Come, stack arms, men; pile on the rails,

Stonewall Jackson

Stir up the campfires bright;
No matter if the canteen fails
We'll make a roaring night.
Here Shenandoah brawls along,
There lofty Blue Ridge echoes strong
To swell the Brigade's roaring song
Of Stonewall Jackson's Way.

We see him now — the old slouched hat
Cocked o'er his eye askew,
The shrewd dry smile, the speech so pat
So calm, so blunt, so true. . . .
He's in the saddle now! Fall in!
Steady, the whole brigade.

Now hear the story of how well he died
Told by our poet, lost to us too soon,
Stephen Vincent Benét, soldier's son,
Who wrote in living words the tragic tale:

*

In the dense heart of the thicketed Wilderness,
Stonewall Jackson lies dying for four long days.
They have cut off his arm,
They have tried such arts as they know,
But no arts now can save him.
                      When he was hit
By the blind chance bullet-spatter from his own lines,

HEROES

In the night, in the darkness, they stole him off from the field
To keep the men from knowing, but the men knew. . . .

                              The night fell too soon.
It is hard to tell your friend from your enemy
In such a night. So he rode too far in advance
And turning back toward his lines, unrecognized,
Was fired upon in the night, in the stumbling darkness.

Later on, they brought him a stately letter from Lee
That said in Lee's gracious way, "You have only lost
Your left arm, I my right."

                              The dour mouth opened:
"Better ten Jacksons should fall than one Lee," it said
And closed again, while the heart went on with its task
Of beating off foolish, unnecessary Death.
The slow time wore. They had to tell him at last
That he must die. The doctors were brave enough,
No doubt, but they looked awhile at the man on the bed
And summoned his wife to do it. So she told him.
He would not believe at first. Then he lay awhile
Silent, while some slow, vast, reversal of skies
Went on in the dying brain. At last he spoke.
"All right," he said.

                              She opened the Bible and read.
It was Spring outside the window, the air was warm,
The rough, plank house was full enough of the Spring.
They had had a good life together, those two middle-aged
Calm people, one reading aloud now, the other silent.
They had passed hard schools. They were in love with each
        other

Stonewall Jackson

And had been for many years. Now that tale was told.
They had been poor and odd, found each other trusty,
Begotten children, prayed, disliked to be parted,
Had family-jokes, known weather and other matters,
Planned for an age: they were famous now, he was dying.

The clock moved on, the delirium began.
The watchers listened, trying to catch the words,
Some awed, one broken-hearted. . . .

And let the broken-hearted one, the wife,
Break in upon our poet for awhile.
Let Mary Anna Jackson tell us now
What thoughts were on her mind that fateful hour:

★

Was his voice wandering back in dreams
To the river of his beloved valley, the Shenandoah,
The river of sparkling waters whose verdant meads and
        groves
He had redeemed from the invader? . . . .
Or was he reaching forward across the River Death
To the golden streets of the Celestial City
And the trees whose leaves are for the healing of the nations?
It was to these that God was bringing him
Through his last battle and victory.

Now let the poet's lines tell how he died:

HEROES

*

The dying man
Went back at first to his battles as soldiers do.
He was pushing a new advance
With the old impatience and skill, over tangled ground,
A cloudy drive that did not move as he willed
Though he had it clear in his mind. They were slow today.
Tell A. P. Hill to push them — push the attack —

Push the attack —
Push the attack —
(Dying out in distance) Push the attack —

Get up the guns!

Get up the guns! —
Get up the guns! —
(Dying out in distance) Get up the guns! — get up the
        guns! —
Get up the guns! —

                    The cloudy assault dispersed.
There were no more cannon. The ground was plain enough
        now.
He lay silent, seeing it so, while the watchers listened.
He had been dying once, but that was a dream.
The ground was plain enough now.

He roused himself and spoke in a different voice.
"Let us cross the river," he said, "and rest under the shade
        of the trees."

Stonewall Jackson

"Let us cross the river and rest under the shade of the
        trees." —
So ends the poem — so ended a life.
And somewhere in the gray-clad dwindling ranks
A soldier-poet grieved for his loved leader:
Private Sidney Lanier spoke for the South,
Saying these words for her lost champion,
And all her sorrowing folk repeated them:

★

.... O hero-life that lit us like the sun!
O hero-words that glittered like the stars
And stood and shone above the gloomy wars
        When the hero-life was done! ....

Along the shining waters of the still canal
From Lynchburg north to weeping Lexington
The funeral barge moved slowly, dripping flowers,
Soft hyacinth, magnolias and crepe myrtle,
Wisteria, mimosa and sweet olive,
Virginia creeper, coral vine, cape jasmine,
The while a people mourned their valiant son
Saying a requiem for him they loved:

★

The muffled drum is beating
There's a sad and solemn tread,
Our banner's draped in mourning

139

HEROES

As it shrouds th'illustrious dead.
Proud forms are bent with sorrow
And all Southern hearts are sore,
The Hero now is sleeping,
Noble Stonewall is no more.

Though more than four score years now stretch between
May blooms as lavish now as she did then.
And in that month the people of our South
Still bring their blossoms — and their pride-filled hearts —
To little mounds where lie their soldier dead;
Still sing their hymns and say their earnest prayers
On their Confederate Memorial Day.
But time has healed the bleeding nation's wounds
And on that day beside them others stand,
Their brothers of the North, the East, the West —
The whole vast union of America.
For Stonewall Jackson *all* our country grieves
And in his deeds all take a solemn pride.
This was a noble life that fires us all.
We swear that victory shall crown our banners,
That we shall never for a moment turn aside
From our great purpose till it shall be gained;
That only when the world is free for freedom,
Shall we at last in peacetime cross the river
And rest — under the shade of the trees.

FAMILY LETTERS

★ 16 ★
Lafayette to his Wife

THE United States has been made by people who came here from somewhere else, mostly Europe, in search of a freedom that all men want. And one of our most-honored American heroes was a certain youthful Gentleman of France.

The very map of America is a memorial to him. Mountain and river and town and college and street bear his name. They remind us of the charming, gallant boy who said that when he first heard of our Revolution, "My heart was enrolled in it."

So when the first of two million American troops set foot on France in 1917, an American officer said simply to the French: "Lafayette, we are here." And the American volunteer flyers in that war called themselves the Lafayette Squadron.

When Lafayette was less than two years old his father was killed at the battle of Minden. The boy's mother died young. At sixteen he was married. He wanted to be a famous soldier: he wanted to avenge his father; and what he heard about the struggle in far-away America made him want to take French help to the Americans. All his prudent advisers in France told him to be careful, mind his own business, keep out of the quarrel, stay at home, stand in line for the honors the Court of Marie Antoinette would pretty certainly have for him. But the youth of nineteen had to decide for himself, and he decided.

He said good-by to his young wife, who was expecting a baby. He went in disguise from Paris to the coast. He sailed secretly from France in the spring of 1777. For more than fifty days at sea he never knew when he might be picked up by a British ship and either imprisoned or else sent back to France in disgrace.

Well, his ship ran the blockade, and in June he was in Charleston, South Carolina. As soon as possible he joined Washington in the field.

At Brandywine, Lafayette was wounded, and he captured the hearts of the Continental Army and the American people. He has owned those hearts ever since. He later became so famous that we sometimes forget he was only a boy when he first came to America.

But let us for once not think of him as most of us do: as a statue of bronze or stone, as a portrait of a hero in a powdered wig and a gold-laced coat.

Let us go back to the youngster Lafayette as he was when he arrived in Charleston.

He was sick of the ocean and the ship. He was excited about Americans and about the town of Charleston. He was already dramatizing himself, this young nobleman, as a citizen of the rising republic. He could not know yet that he was to be adopted almost as a son by Washington; nor that he was to be made an honorary American citizen; nor that every one of his direct male descendants, down to our own time, was to be a citizen both of France and of the United States. Lafayette was only a new volunteer come to help us.

The grandees of Charleston had just given a dinner for him, and it had lasted five hours. He was tired now, and homesick. Back in his room at last, he sat down to write to Adrienne — a letter from a soldier overseas to his wife, waiting for their child.

★

My last letter to you, my dear love, has informed you, that I arrived safely in this country, after suffering a little from sea-sickness during the first weeks of the voyage; that I was then, the morning after I landed, at the home of a very kind officer; that I had been nearly two months on the passage, and that I wished to set off immediately. It spoke of everything most interesting to my heart; of my sorrow at parting from you, and of our dear children; and it said, besides, that I was in excellent health. . . .

I have such confidence in my lucky star that I hope it will reach you. This same star has befriended me, to the astonishment of everybody here. Trust to it yourself, and be assured that it ought to calm all your fears. I landed after having sailed several days along a coast which swarmed with hostile vessels. . . .

I will now tell you about the country and its inhabitants. They are as agreeable as my enthusiasm had painted them.

Lafayette to his Wife

Simplicity of manners, kindness, love of country and of liberty, and a delightful equality everywhere prevail. The wealthiest man and the poorest are on a level; and, although there are some large fortunes, I challenge any one to discover the slightest difference between these two classes respectively towards each other. . . .

The city of Charleston is one of the handsomest and best built, and its inhabitants among the most agreeable, that I have ever seen. The American women are very pretty, simple in their manners, and exhibit a neatness, which is everywhere cultivated even more studiously than in England. What most charms me is, that all the citizens are brethren.

In America, there are no poor, nor even what we call peasantry. Each individual has his own honest property, and the same rights as the most wealthy landed proprietor. The inns are very different from those of Europe; the host and hostess sit at table with you, and do the honors of a comfortable meal; and, on going away, you pay your bill without haggling. When one does not wish to go to an inn, there are country-houses where the title of a good American is a sufficient passport to all those civilities paid in Europe to one's friend . . . .

Considering the pleasant life I lead in this country, my sympathy with the people, which makes me feel as much at ease in their society as if I had known them for twenty years, the similarity between their mode of thinking and my own, and my love of liberty and glory — one might suppose that I am very happy.

But you are not with me; my friends are not with me; and there is no happiness for me far from you and them. I ask you, if you still love me; but I put the same question much oftener to myself, and my heart always responds, Yes. I am impatient beyond measure to hear from you. I hope to find letters at Philadelphia. My only fear is that the privateer, which is to bring them, may be captured on her passage . . . .

Write frequently, and long letters. You do not know the full extent of the joy with which I shall receive them . . . . May I say, embrace tenderly our children? The father of those poor children is a rover, but a good and honest man at heart; a good father, who loves his family dearly, and good husband, who loves his wife with all his heart. . . . .

Remember me to your friends and my own . . . .

I must leave off for want of paper and time; and if I do not repeat to you ten thousand times that I love you, it is not from any want of feeling, but from modesty; since I have the presumption to hope that I have already convinced you of it. The night is far advanced, and the heat dreadful. I am devoured by insects; so, you see, the best countries have their disadvantages. Adieu.

LAFAYETTE

Narcissa Whitman

ONE of the most valiant of all Americans was a woman. She was born Narcissa Prentiss at Angelica, New York. She was one of the first pupils at Emma Willard's pioneering Seminary at Troy. She was gentle, delicately brought up, surrounded with comfort and conveniences.

Then she married Marcus Whitman in February 1836. Whitman was a medical missionary in Oregon. His bride was to spend her honeymoon in a covered wagon, roughing it for the first time in her life. She gave up her friends, her books, her comfort to go to a country that was not even part of the United States. She was never to return.

Before Narcissa Whitman no white woman had crossed this continent. Her trip proved that women could cross from East to West. She left one of our cherished human documents: a diary which gives, day by day, a picture of what it meant to cross the rivers, plains and mountains of America, by wagon:

★

Our manner of living is far preferable to any in the States. I never was so contented and happy before; neither have I enjoyed such health for years. As soon as the day breaks, the first that we hear is the words "Arise! Arise!" Then the mules set up such a noise as you never heard, which puts the whole camp in motion. You must think it very hard to get up so early after sleeping on the ground, when you find it hard work to open your eyes at seven o'clock. Just think of me. Every morning at the word "Arise!" we all spring. While the horses are feeding, we get breakfast in a hurry, and eat it. By this time the words "Catch up! Catch up!" ring through the camp for moving. We are ready to start usually at six, travel till eleven, encamp, rest and feed, start again about two, travel until six, or before, if we come to a good camp-ground, then encamp for the night . . . .

How do you think we manage to rest ourselves every noon, having no house to shelter us from the scorching heat? Perhaps you think we always encamp in the shade of some thick wood. Such a sight I have not seen, lo these many days. If we can find a few small willows or a single lone tree, we think ourselves amply provided for. But often our camping places are in some open plain, and frequently a sand plain. But even here is rest and comfort. My husband, who is one of the best the world ever knew, is always ready to provide a comfortable shade, with one of our saddle blankets spread upon some willows, or sticks placed in the ground. How do you think you would like this?

Just take a peep at us while we are sitting at meals. Our table is the ground, our table cloth is an India-rubber cloth used, when it rains, as a cloak. Our dishes are made of tin, basins for tea cups, iron spoons and plates for each of us, and several pans for milk and to put our meat in when we wish to set it on the table. Each one carries his own knife in his scabbard, and it is always ready for use. When the table things are spread, after making our own forks of sticks, we gather round the table.

Narcissa Whitman

Twelve miles a day was the prescribed distance to be made. The flour soon gave out, and bread was no longer available. The men and women lived on buffalo meat, and occasional berries. There were no roads, and no bridges. What few rude sign posts there were pointed in only one direction — westward.

One day the Whitman party came to the Snake River. Whitman decided he could take only one wagon with him to the Columbia. Narcissa had to give up the one possession in the world that was her own. We know what it cost her from this letter to her sister:

*

Dear Harriet: The little trunk you gave me has come with me so far, and now I must leave it here alone.

Poor little trunk, I am sorry to leave thee. Thou must abide here alone, and no more by thy presence remind me of my dear Harriet. Twenty miles below the falls on Snake River — this shall be thy place of rest. Farewell, little trunk! I thank thee for all thy faithful services, and that I have been cheered by thy presence so long. Thus we scatter as we go.

The hills are so steep and rocky that my husband thought it best to lighten the wagon as much as possible, and take nothing but the wheels, leaving the wagon box with my trunk. I regret leaving everything that came from home, especially this trunk; but it is best. It would have been better for me not to have attempted to bring any baggage whatever, only what was necessary for use on the way. To pack and unpack so many times, and cross so many streams when the packs frequently get wet, requires no small amount of labor, besides the injury of the articles. Our books, what few we have, have been wet several times. The custom of the country is to possess nothing, and then you will lose nothing while traveling.

Early in September they reached the Columbia, near Fort Walla Walla, and found green vegetables from the fort's garden more exciting than gold. As soon as they could build it, they had a house: . . . . of one room. Blankets covered the windows. Green cotton-wood branches spread on the floor made their bed. There was no furniture.

For eleven years they maintained the mission station they had come west to serve. They were the first of the stream that followed them into Oregon. In 1847 came tragedy: measles struck down white children and Indian. Whitman's medicines cured the white children but had no effect on the Indians. The story spread that he was poisoning them. Angry Indians massacred the Whitmans.

But they had lived long enough to point the way. And in one of Narcissa Whitman's letters we find a few, simple words that reveal the spirit of all Americans who have helped to make our Scriptures:

★

Sometimes my wicked heart has been disposed to murmur,

thinking I should have no rest from the heat when we stopped. But I have always been reproved for it by the comfort and rest received. Under the circumstances I have never wished to go back. Such a thought never finds a place in my heart. "The Lord is better to us than our fears." I always find it so.

★ 18 ★

The Naturalization of Jack Roberts

Once there was a German whose desire to be an American took him round the world and through a prison.

★

. . . . I would go around the world again if necessary . . . . but sooner or later I would make my home in the United States. I was held in San Pedro, California. My room was a cell with iron bars for windows, separating me from my fellowmen. But this did not dim the beauty of this country for me, nor lessen my determination to make America my home.

These are the words of Jack Roberts, who was a sergeant in the Army Air Force when he wrote them. They are from a letter he wrote on a day that seemed to him the most important of his life. His letter was written that evening to some friends who knew only a part of his story:

★

Pine Camp, New York
July 1942.
Dear Friends: Today I am so very happy. Something won-

The Naturalization of Jack Roberts

derful occurred and I am so overjoyed that I feel I must share the great news with all of you. For on this day I have realized a great longing . . . I became an American citizen.

Does it surprise you to hear an American soldier talk of becoming an American citizen? But that had happened to Jack Roberts. For he had been born in Germany, with a German name which he has reason to use no longer, had hated the Nazis, and had left his native land in search of safety and liberty elsewhere — in Australia, in China, or as a seaman on the ships of free countries. Then in 1938 — but let Jack Roberts tell his story in his own words:

*

It was the year 1938 when I entered this country. I had to fight for my entry and finally won. But at first I was almost deported. Making up my mind to remain in this country and apply for citizenship, I tried many channels, and the reply was always the same. If a seaman enters this country as a foreign seaman and is granted a sixty-day stay, there is no way of changing his status unless he leaves the United States, goes to the nearest country which will admit him, and applies for legal entry from that country.

I had lived in Australia for a short while. So that was my "nearest country," and there I would be admitted.

I could not find a ship sailing direct to Australia, so I accepted a job on a small Norwegian ship sailing for Oslo, Norway — an unusual way to travel to Australia! We went from Oslo to Hamburg, Rotterdam, Antwerp, then around South Australia to Sydney. The day we arrived, after fifty-four days at sea, I saw the American consul and made my application.

Months passed before I was finally given a quota number and received a visa. During those months in Australia I spent my savings and had to keep myself going by working as a painter, salesman, or whatever jobs were available. Then I learned of a ship sailing to California, and I worked my way through on it. I landed in California on October 12, 1938 — Columbus Day.

To my consternation, a technical error was found in my papers, and the authorities informed me that I had the choice of either being deported back to Australia on the same ship, or of being detained for an indefinite period, until my case came up for a hearing in Washington. So I was detained. The immigration officers were sympathetic when they learned about my trip around the world. One of them actually shook my hand when I told him that if I should have to wait twelve months and then be deported, I would go around the world again if necessary — but sooner or later I would make my home in the United States of America.

So Jack Roberts, who had worked his way round the world to become an American citizen, was now willing to be confined while he waited, with no way of knowing how long he might have to wait:

I was held in San Pedro, California. My room was a cell with iron bars for windows, separating me from my fellowmen. But this did not dim the beauty of this country for me, nor lessen my determination to make America my home. Most unexpectedly, on October 22, only ten days later, a decision came from Washington, allowing my entry into the country, and I was set free. I said good-bye to the officials and walked out a free man, with a boiling emotion in my heart.

Of course he had still to wait for his naturalization to be completed. He went to sea again, in the merchant marine, and was a radio operator at the time of Pearl Harbor. In February he joined the Army, in May he was transferred to Pine Camp, New York. There in July he became a citizen. That was the day he wrote his exultant letter to his friends, soon after he came back to the barracks from the courtroom where he had sworn the oath of allegiance.

★

I entered the courtroom. There were many soldiers, men in uniform already defending the country which was about to adopt them. The clerk called our names and we came forward, lining up and facing the judge.

There were eighty of us: Eriksens, DeSilvos, Gottfrieds — men from Scandinavia, the Balkans, Portugal, Germany, Ireland, Scotland. We faced the colors, we raised our right hands. It was quiet in the courtroom. A great drama was taking place — a world drama represented in each and every one of us. Some of the boys had only recently arrived or escaped from the other side.

The judge administered the oath and the men repeated the words after him:

*

I hereby declare on oath, that I absolutely and entirely renounce and abjure all allegiance and fidelity to any foreign prince, potentate, state or sovereignty of whom or which I have heretofore been a subject or citizen; that I will support and defend the Constitution and laws of the United States against all enemies, foreign and domestic; that I will bear true faith and allegiance to the same; and that I take this obligation freely, without any mental reservation or purpose of evasion: So help me God!

As we repeated the oath after the judge, his and our voices seemed suddenly to roar in the courtroom, as if challenging the whole world against any attempt to touch us or divide us, or to get close to the flag around which we all stood and the ideals for which it stands.

As we pronounced every word, we felt and knew that for us Bataan had not fallen, that Wake Island will be avenged, that Madrid, Warsaw, Oslo, Rotterdam, Paris, Prague, Belgrade, Brussels, Athens, Nanking, and Sevastopol will see the flags of liberty flying again.

The oath of allegiance ended, and it was very quiet for a few seconds. Then the judge spoke to us. He congratulated us heartily on becoming American citizens. Then, very thoughtfully, the judge looked at us and spoke again.

"I would like to say a few more words to you, and not as a judge, but as a soldier to soldiers and as a father of a soldier. I fought in the last war, and my son is serving now with the

The Naturalization of Jack Roberts

Fifth Armored Division. Some of you will see action soon, probably. You will meet a brutal enemy, a strong enemy. Fight! fight! for you are the salvation of the world for many years to come. You will win. And we here, not in uniform, will do our share to help you. So God bless you and take care of you."

His voice sounded unsteady, very unsteady. He turned abruptly and left us.

Outside the sun was shining, and the noise of busy traffic could be heard through the windows. I could hear the voices and see the activities of Americans on the job. I drew my sleeve across my eyes to clear my vision, and the smell of powder on my hand reminded me of the rifle range. I walked out quickly. I also had a job. I am an American!

This is the story of what one man did to become a citizen of this country, and of what that meant to him. How many of us, who were born citizens, have taken our citizenship for granted, without a thought of what it means! But now how few of us, who have heard these words from Jack Roberts, can help feeling a swift rush of pride to our hearts, and in our minds a fresh determination to bear true faith and allegiance.

OPENING OF THE CONTINENT

Under the circumstances, I have never wished to go back.

—Narcissa Whitman

PLATE TWENTY-FIVE

THE COVERED WAGON

PAINTED BY SAMUEL COLEMAN. COURTESY OF HALL PARK MCCULLOUGH AND THE
METROPOLITAN MUSEUM OF ART, NEW YORK CITY.

160

The commands of democracy are as imperative as its privileges and opportunities are wide and generous.

— WOODROW WILSON

PLATE TWENTY-SIX

VERDICT OF THE PEOPLE, 1854

PAINTED BY GEORGE CALEB BINGHAM. COURTESY OF THE BOATMEN'S NATIONAL BANK OF ST. LOUIS, ST. LOUIS, MISSOURI.

162

163

. . . *ideals are like stars; you will not succeed in touching them with your hands.*

— CARL SCHURZ

PLATE TWENTY-SEVEN

THE NANTUCKET SCHOOL OF PHILOSOPHY

PAINTED BY EASTMAN JOHNSON. COURTESY OF THE WALTER'S ART GALLERY, BALTIMORE, MARYLAND.

This is the sacred mystery of democracy, that its richest fruits spring up out of soils which no man has prepared.

— WOODROW WILSON

PLATE TWENTY-EIGHT

SUNDAY MORNING

PAINTED BY EASTMAN JOHNSON. OWNED BY THE NEW-YORK HISTORICAL SOCIETY, NEW YORK CITY.

166

167

There is no where in the land any home so remote, so humble that it may not contain the power of mind and heart and conscience to which . . . history submits its process.

— WOODROW WILSON

168

In the days when water was the greatest highway, the citizens of the United States bound themselves and the world together.

PLATE THIRTY

LEVEE AT NEW ORLEANS, 1883

PAINTED BY W. A. WALKER. COURTESY OF THE BLAND GALLERY, NEW YORK CITY.

171

... the people of our South. Still bring their blossoms—and their pride-filled hearts—to little mounds where lie their soldier dead.

172

Be it ever so humble, there's no place like home.

—JOHN HOWARD PAYNE

PLATE THIRTY-TWO

RETURNING TO THE FARM

PAINTED BY G. H. DURRIE, OWNED BY THE NEW-YORK HISTORICAL SOCIETY, NEW YORK CITY.

174

★ 19 ★

George Rogers Clark

MANY of us do not realize that when we were fighting for our independence, Detroit was strongly held by the enemy, who threatened the old Northwest that is now the Middle West. Far from being our Middle West then, it was a part of the Province of Quebec, which reached below the Great Lakes, south to the Ohio and west to the Mississippi. The United States was only a strip of settlements along the Atlantic seaboard from Canada to Florida. Most of the Indians of the inland territory were allied with the British. And the British had forts not only at Detroit but also at Kaskaskia on the Mississippi and at Vincennes on the Wabash.

There were no American defenders of that inland territory except the Kentuckians south of the Ohio. A little Kentucky Army, under the command of George Rogers Clark, marched in 1778 against the enemy posts at Kaskaskia and Vincennes and captured them. An enemy expedition from Detroit recaptured Vincennes. The news reached Clark at Kaskaskia. Then followed, in the icy month of February 1779, one of the most valiant military exploits in American history.

OPENING OF THE CONTINENT

The world has always loved the tales of men
Who stood against the gods of circumstance,
Daring to wager life's bright shining coin
On one forlorn and desperate enterprise,
Fighting their way to its becurtained end.
Such men were those whom we remember now
With proud and grateful thoughts but halting words,
For language fails when we would bid it tell
The greatness of their deed — or of their hearts.

Now let the sunlight of a distant day
Slant on the Mississippi's yellow flood
Save where a sharp black shadow slides along,
A trim canoe, swift paddled toward the shore.
So Francis Vigo, Spanish fur merchant,
Sped to the landing at Kaskaskia
And shouted as he came: "Vincennes has fallen!
The British tyrant has regained Vincennes."
A moment later Vigo clasped the hand
Of him he sought, a giant of a man,
Red-headed, black-eyed, lean — George Rogers Clark,
Commander of the Continental troops,
Three score and ten Kentuckians, that held
The town — and he but twenty-five years old.
The Spaniard told George Clark about a letter
That Captain Leonard Helm had written him,
Sitting alone within the fort at St. Vincennes,
And looking through an open porthole down
Upon the red-coats marching toward its gates.
(His messenger had not escaped their lines
But Clark and Vigo guessed what Helm had said.)
And we who can look on the level past,
Standing a moment on a rise in ground

George Rogers Clark

That history sometimes gives can see the truth
That lies upon its fading crumpled page.
The captain little knew in his despair
That — writing in great haste — he dipped his pen
In shining ink of immortality.
But *we* know — we are proud to claim his note
Among the treasured Scriptures of our past.
And we may bid him march time's lengthening road,
Threading the fields of our imaginings
That we may hear the words he meant for Clark.

*

Dear Sir:

At this time there is an army within three miles of this
place. I heard of their coming several days beforehand. I
sent spies to find the certainty. The spies being taken prisoners
I never got intelligence till they got within three miles of
the town. . . .

There is a break in the letter, after that,
For there were duties Captain Helm must do
Before returning to his pen again.

*

Excuse haste as the army is in sight. My determination is
to defend the Garrison, though I have but twenty-one men.
The army is in three hundred yards of the village. You

must think how I feel; not four men that I can really depend on, but am determined to act brave.

Think of my condition. I know it is out of my power to defend the town.

Their flag is at a small distance. I must conclude.

Your humble servant,
Leonard Helm.

Brave Leonard Helm was taken prisoner —
So Francis Vigo told George Rogers Clark —
And one week later, February fifth
Of 1779, Clark marched away,
Leaving Kaskaskia, to retake Vincennes.
And sixty Frenchmen, pledging loyalty
To their new country's flag, were joined with him,
To trudge beside the rifles of Kentucky.
All of the hundred and thirty knew they faced
Two hundred miles of flooded prairie land
Before they reached the fort they meant to take.
Two weeks they marched through water and through rain.
The mud sucked at their boots, but they kept on,
Shouting and singing, hunting along the way,
Fording the streams and laughing at a boy —
A playful drummer floating on his drum,
Until they heard, far off, a morning cannon
And saw a wall of water, shoulder-deep,
Spread out for mile on mile across the land.
They plunged into it, marched till day was done,
Sleeping all wet and cold, on barren islands
(Green hilltops once, in summer long ago),
Cheering each other on with songs and jesting

Until their food was gone. Yet on they slogged,
Lifting one foot from mud to flowing water,
Setting it down to sink in thickening ooze.
Clinging to trees, to rocks, and to each other,
Stung by long chilling rains, they staggered on.
This was a march such as no men had endured
Since time began, a march to win a land,
To claim the drowned plains and the hills beyond
For union with the thirteen starry states
Fighting their way to freedom from a king.
The third long week began, all hope seemed gone.
But Captain Joseph Bowman kept his journal
And set down notes on three heroic days
The while he dried himself beside the fires
That flared on the little island hills:

★

February 21st:
We thought to get to town that night, so plunged into the
water, sometimes to the neck for more than one league when
we stopped, there being no dry land near us on one side for
many leagues. Our pilots say we cannot get along, that it was
impossible. Rain all this day; no provisions.
February 22nd:
Colonel Clark encouraged his men which gave them great
spirits. Marched on in the water, those that were weak and
fainted from so much fatigue went in the canoes. We came
one league further to some sugar camps, where we staid all
night. Heard the evening and morning guns from the Fort.
No provisions yet. Lord help us!
February 23rd:

OPENING OF THE CONTINENT

Set off to cross a plain, called Horse Shoe Plain, about four miles long covered with water breast high. Here we expected some of our brave men must certainly perish, having froze in the night, and so long fasting, and no other resource but wading this plain or rather *lake* of water. We pushed in with courage, Colonel Clark being the first, taking care to have the boats close by to take those that was weak and benumbed into them. About one o'clock we came in sight of the town.

George Rogers Clark, himself, described the hour
The long march ended. Let the red-haired colonel
Relate the story, scarce to be believed:

★

The men exerted themselves beyond their abilities — the weak holding by the stronger. But the water never got shallower but continued deepening. Getting to the woods where they expected land the water was up to my shoulders. All the low men and weakly hung to the trees and floated on the old logs until they were taken off by the canoes. The strong and tall got ashore and built fires. Many would reach the shore and fall with their bodies half in the water.

Crossing a narrow deep lake we came to a copse of timber called the Warrior's Island. We were now in full view of the fort and town. Every man now feasted his eyes and forgot that he had suffered anything, agreeing that all that had passed was owing to a good policy and nothing but what a man could bear.

George Rogers Clark

That night before the fort the war drums beat
And Clark's men lay in shadow of the walls
Firing a rain that quickened the torches' flare
When enemy gunners sought to fire their cannon.
And in the morning the white flag of truce
Fluttered in sunlight — and Vincennes was won!
Vincennes was won — and all the prairie west!
No alien would ever dare again
Claim any grain of sand of the Great Lakes shores.
Ohio, Indiana, Michigan,
Wisconsin, Illinois — were ours forever.
The Northwest Territory had been taken
By seventy bold sons of bright Kentucky
And sixty Creole Frenchmen, comrades all.

So sons of liberty throughout the world
Have fought, and still do fight for rights that men
Who scorn to live as whimpering slaves demand.
Kaskaskia and Vincennes are golden names.
Our hearts repeat them with a solemn pride.
The struggle, now as then, remains the same.
Wherever even justice is assailed
Strong men will rise as in the years gone by,
And all the hardships that they may endure
Though death should be the final sacrifice
Shall be "nothing but what a man could bear."

Erie Canal

SOMETIMES, in the vast present in which we live, with its mighty armies and navies, the thunderous power of its machines, the swiftness of its movements and communications—we find ourselves thinking of the past as small and weak and slow in comparison. Marathon seems a little thing beside Stalingrad, or the surrender at Saratoga beside the landing in Normandy. And yet those ancient battles changed the course of history as truly as modern battles have. And in all history there have been many small episodes of peace that were the seeds of whole great futures.

In one such prophetic episode the Great Lakes were joined to the Atlantic Ocean. Water from rivers everywhere in the world were poured symbolically into the harbor of New York.

On a brisk fall day a hundred and nineteen years ago the first craft ever to travel by water from the inland seas we call the Great Lakes to the Atlantic Ocean entered the new Erie Canal. As the packet *Seneca Chief* floated into the waters of the man-made channel, the cannon of a battery hundreds of miles long began to fire.

Stationed at emplacements within earshot of each other, the great guns boomed out the news that the vast forests and woods of America had found outlet to the sea.

Erie Canal

The cannoneers of Rochester heard thunder in the West and yanked lanyards. The Syracuse gunners sped the great news on over the hills to Utica. Through the valley of the Mohawk the sound surged on toward the Hudson. There it turned southward and, racing between the mountains, echoing against the walls of the Palisades, it finally reached New York. In eighty-one minutes the first news ever carried on sound-waves for over five hundred miles—had arrived.

For eight years the people of America had awaited this moment. Now the East and West were one. The furs of the northwest woods might now find markets across the seas. The tall timbers of Michigan, the grains of Ohio could float to eastern ports.

Let the waters of time recede for a moment. Let the ripples of the years give way and let us stand beside the stone aqueduct at Rochester in western New York as the *Seneca Chief* approaches. Waiting to swing in behind her lies the packet *Young Lion of the West*. In cages on her deck are two eagles, two wolves, a fawn, a fox and four raccoons — symbols of the union of wilderness and city, which the canal has consummated. Hear the conversation as it took place between the captains of the packets and the officers of the city on October 26, 1825:

"Who comes there?"

"Your brothers from the West, on the waters of the Great Lakes."

"By what means have they been diverted so far from their natural course?"

"Through the channel of the Erie Canal."

"By whose authority and by whom was a work of such magnitude accomplished?"

OPENING OF THE CONTINENT

"By the authority and by the enterprise of the people of the State of New York."

The people of the United States waited as the parade of packets moved on west — then south. At Albany a great fleet of white steamboats, elaborate floating palaces, waited to join the line. Along the banks of the Hudson, the people of the river towns celebrated the passing of the water-parade with sky-borne fireworks and blazing bonfires. The West was moving to the East. A man-made stream had united the trappers and the farmers of the West with the merchants of the East in one brotherhood. Across the wide oceans of the world other peoples awaited the products of the heart of America.

It was a sunny Saturday morning, the fourth of November, when the steamboat *Washington*, moving up the Hudson, met the parading fleet from the West. Then the men on her decks heard the hail that signalized a greater unity than our country had ever known:

"Whence come ye?"
"An escort from Lake Erie."
"Whither bound?"
"To the Atlantic — what vessel is that?"
"*The Yacht of the City of New York* — to welcome you into our waters, congratulate you on the great event, and offer the hospitalities of the City."

Out into the bay the great convoy moved in sunlight. There, just inside Sandy Hook, the vessels moved into a great circle three miles in circumference. On board the *Seneca Chief*, the tall, majestic Governor of New York, De Witt Clinton, was seeing his great dream come true. Long years of planning

186

Erie Canal

and eight years of building were now at an end. Clinton's Ditch — as his enemies had called it — was now the Erie Canal. The Governor lifted a bright green keg ringed with gilded hoops and held it over the side. Sparkling, the waters of Lake Erie fell from the keg into the ocean. Then in all humility at the hour of his triumph De Witt Clinton said:

★

May the God of the heavens and the earth smile most propitiously on this work . . . . and may he render it subservient to the best interests of the human race.

And when Governor Clinton had finished speaking, the learned American scientist, Dr. Samuel Latham Mitchell, opened phial after phial of the waters of the rivers of the world into New York bay. Drop by glittering drop the waters of the Elbe, the Ganges, the Nile, the Amazon, the Neva, the Plata, the Tagus, the Orinoco, the Seine, the Thames — united with the ocean below as symbols "of our commercial intercourse with all ports of the world."

So, in the days when water was the greatest of the highways of travel, the citizens of the United States bound themselves and the world together. De Witt Clinton wished the canal to serve the human race. Samuel Mitchell wished it to be a symbol of the triumph of democracy, which all the world might read. Today, when we know that the highway of the future is the air, when we know that the argosies of tomorrow shall be great liners and great freighters cleaving the skies of all the world — we once again pledge ourselves to the principles for which the men of our past stood.

Ever mindful of the equality and the brotherhood of men, we repeat once more our desire that these United States shall serve not only themselves as one great nation, but all nations who look forward with us to the day of peaceful commerce throughout the world. Our goal today, as in the past, is not to serve ourselves but all the world,

★ 21 ★

The Transcontinental Railway

THOMAS HART BENTON was a United States Senator from Missouri in the days of the covered wagon and the California Gold Rush.

Senator Benton seemed visionary to many people then, because he fought for something that we now take for granted. He fought for a transcontinental railroad—beyond Chicago and St. Louis to the Pacific. And with far-reaching vision he foresaw that railways from coast to coast would some day join the seas which separate America from those older worlds, the world of Europe and the world of Asia.

In a Convention Hall in St. Louis Senator Benton spoke prophetic words:

★

Three and a half centuries ago the great Columbus . . . . in the year 1492 departed from Europe to arrive in the East by going to the West. It was a sublime conception . . . . Two continents, not dreamed of before, arrested his voyage to India.

In the beginning, and in barbarous ages, the sea was a barrier to the intercourse of nations. It separated nations . . . . Mechanical genius, in inventing the ship, converted that barrier into a facility. The land and continents became the

189

obstructions . . . . Now in our day, mechanical genius has again triumphed over the obstacles of nature . . . .

The steam car has worked upon the land . . . . among enlightened nations the miracle which the ship in barbarous ages worked upon the ocean. The land has now become the facility for the most distant communications . . . . We hold the intervening land; we hold the obstacle which stopped Columbus; we are in the line between Europe and Asia.

We have it in our power to remove that obstacle . . . . and to carry him on to his land of promise and hope, with a rapidity, a precision, and a safety unknown to all ocean navigation. A king and a queen started him upon his great enterprise. It lies in the hands of a republic to complete it. It lies in our hands.

We the people of the United States, of this first half of this nineteenth century, let us raise ourselves. Let us rise to the grandeur of the occasion. Let us complete the grand design of Columbus, by putting Europe and Asia into communication, and that to our advantage, through the heart of our country. Let us give to his ships, converted into cars, a continued course, unknown to all former times. Let us make the iron road, and make it from sea to sea.

Let us now, in this convention, rise above everything sectional, personal, local. Let us beseech the national legislature to build the great road upon the great national line which unites Europe and Asia — the line which will find, on our continent, the Bay of San Francisco at one end, and the national metropolis and great commercial emporiums at the other.

And let it be adorned with its crowning honor, the colossal statute of the great Columbus, whose design it accomplishes, hewn from the granite mass of a peak of the Rocky Mountains, overlooking the road — the mountain itself the ped-

estal, and the statue a part of the mountain, pointing with out-
stretched hand to the western horizon, and saying to the
flying messenger: There is the East. There is India.

Thus Benton made his great plea for a railroad across America. We take such railroads as a matter of course today, but
twenty years passed between the day of that speech and the
day when the first railway line all the way from coast to coast
was finished. Mountains had to be vanquished; deserts de-
feated; rivers spanned. Foot by hard-won foot, mile by
back-breaking mile, the railroad crept from Omaha west,
and from Sacramento east.

Then at Promontory Point at the northern end of the
shores of Great Salt Lake came the meeting of the lines. It
was a cold bright day in May, 1869. Two trains, one from
the east, one from the west faced each other across a little gap
in the track. About six hundred people were looking on. Officials from New York and San Francisco. Workers swarming
on top of the two trains. A few Indians, Mexicans. Some
soldiers in uniform. A photographer ready with his cameras.
And telegraphers at their keys, ready to flash the news to
both oceans.

The final tie was laid — polished laurel from California,
with a silver plate commemorating the day. Chinese workmen
in their best clothes brought up the last rail and put it in
place. A clergyman from Massachusetts offered an invoca-
tion. The band of the 21st Infantry played *America*.

OPENING OF THE CONTINENT

And then the last spike, of California gold. Leland Stanford, governor of the state and president of the Central Pacific, stood there, frock-coated, high-hatted, bearded, with a silver sledge. The telegrapher's hand was on his key. At each blow on the last spike he was to send a signal, so that the whole nation could share the ceremony.

Governor Stanford swung his sledge — and missed. Men who had driven spikes over all the miles from Omaha and Sacramento roared with laughter. But the alert telegrapher sent the signal anyway. The driving went on. Thomas Durant of New York, representing the Union Pacific, wearing a velvet coat, also swung the sledge. The two locomotives drew slowly up till their cowcatchers almost touched. The engineers climbed out and shook hands. Then each of them broke a bottle of champagne over the other's engine. The crowd shouted, the band played, the locomotive whistles drowned out all the other sounds.

But there was more to the ceremony than the small crowd at Promontory Point could see. For the telegraph made the ceremony nation-wide. At the signal a magnetic ball dropped on the pole on the dome of the Capitol at Washington. Bells rang in Independence Hall in Philadelphia. There was a salute of a hundred guns in City Hall Park in New York. In Chicago crowds fell into a volunteer procession, seven miles long. San Francisco, which had already been celebrating for two days, carried an exultant banner through the streets saying that "California Annexes the United States."

The Transcontinental Railway

This was probably the most important and most exciting non-military ceremony in the whole history of the American people. For it was railroads that did most to make the states, from east to west, united. Those early dreamers are gone but the railroads remain.

MONUMENTS

Liberty Bell

THERE IS an old poem which a great many American children used to know, and many of them by heart. Perhaps some children now do not know the poem as their grandfathers and grandmothers used to know it, and still do. But the children of our day will find the story still as exciting as it ever seemed to the earlier generations of American children who loved it.

The story takes place in the old city of Philadelphia in 1751, twenty-five years before the signing of the Declaration of Independence. The people of the city wanted a bell to hang in the steeple of the State House of the Colony of Pennsylvania. A man who loved liberty and believed in independence was made chairman of a committee to buy the new bell. His name was Isaac Norris. Isaac Norris ordered the bell from a bell-maker in London, and just to let the people know how he felt about the rights of men, he chose a verse from the Bible to be emblazoned in letters of bronze round the bell's crown:

★

From the Book of Leviticus, the twenty-fifth chapter, the tenth verse: "Proclaim liberty throughout all the land unto all the inhabitants thereof."

196

Liberty Bell

When the bell was delivered in Philadelphia it was hung in the steeple of the red brick State House and tried out. At the first stroke of its clapper it cracked. It was taken down and sent to two American bell-makers who re-melted it and made it over twice before they were satisfied with its tone. Then it was put back in the steeple. There it was hanging on June 7, 1776 when, behind the closed doors down below, a man rose to speak before the Continental Congress. A year had passed since the days of Paul Revere's ride, the fight at Lexington, the Battle of Bunker Hill. The faces of the congressmen were worried and thoughtful as Richard Henry Lee of Virginia read out a resolution which he wanted them to vote upon. Listen and you will hear an echo of his voice as it filled the big room in the State House where the Congress was meeting:

★

Resolved: That the United Colonies are and ought to be free and independent states.

There were days of argument after that, for many thought it was not yet time for the colonies to declare their independence. While the debate was going on a committe was appointed to draw up a formal declaration.

Benjamin Franklin and John Adams, members of that committee, persuaded Thomas Jefferson, young, tall, red-headed, to do the writing, with a few words changed or added by the other two.

MONUMENTS

*

When, in the course of human events, it becomes necessary for one people to dissolve the political bands that have connected them with another, and to assume, among the powers of the earth, the separate and equal station to which the laws of nature and of nature's God entitle them, a decent respect to the opinions of mankind requires that they should declare the causes which impel them to this separation.

We hold these truths to be self-evident, that all men are created equal; that they are endowed by their Creator with certain unalienable rights; that among these are life, liberty, and the pursuit of happiness. That to secure these rights, governments are instituted among men, deriving their just powers from the consent of the governed; . . . .

And now it is July 4, 1776. The Congress is in session and a rumor has spread among the people that behind those closed doors of the State House the Congress may vote upon a declaration of independence. Let the American Scripture which is the old poem tell the rest.

It is based on early tradition. The men who write history point out that while the Declaration of Independence was adopted on July 4th, it was not given out to the people of Philadelphia until July 8th. But countless American children have chosen to believe the story that the poem tells.

In all of the little red schoolhouses that used to dot this great land of ours it was a favorite piece for boys and girls to speak on Friday afternoons. Here, then, told in verse, is the story of an old man, a little boy, and a big bell, the bell that still may be found in the old State House — now called

Liberty Bell

Independence Hall — the cracked old bell all Americans
love — the Liberty Bell:

★

There was a tumult in the city,
In the quaint old Quaker town,
And the streets were rife with people
Pacing restless up and down —
People gathering at corners,
Where they whispered each to each,
And the sweat stood on their temples
With the earnestness of speech.

As the bleak Atlantic currents
Lash the wild Newfoundland shore,
So they beat against the State House,
So they surged against the door;
And the mingling of their voices
Made the harmony profound,
Till the quiet street of Chestnut
Was all turbulent with sound.

Will they do it? Dare they do it?
Who is speaking? What's the news?
What of Adams? What of Sherman?
Oh, God grant they won't refuse!
Make some way there! Let me nearer.
I am stifling! Stifle then!
When a nation's life's at hazard
We've no time to think of men!

199

MONUMENTS

So they surged again the State House,
While all solemnly inside,
Sat the Continental Congress,
Truth and reason for their guide,
O'er a simple scroll debating,
Which, though simple it might be,
Yet should shake the cliffs of England
With the thunders of the free.

Far aloft in that high steeple
Sat the bellman, old and gray,
He was weary of the tyrant
And his iron-sceptered sway;
So he sat, with one hand ready
On the clapper of the bell,
When his eye could catch the signal,
The long-expected news to tell.

See! See! The dense crowd quivers
Through all its lengthy line,
As the boy beside the portal
Hastens forth to give the sign!
With his little hands uplifted,
Breezes dallying with his hair,
Hark! With deep, clear intonation,
Breaks his young voice on the air.

Hushed the people's swelling murmur
Whilst the boy cries joyously:
"Ring! Grandpapa,
Ring! Oh ring for Liberty!"
Quickly at the given signal
The old bellman lifts his hand,

Liberty Bell

Forth he sends the good news, making
Iron music through the land.

How they shouted! What rejoicing!
How the old bell shook the air,
Till the clang of freedom ruffled
The calmly gliding Delaware!
How the bonfires and the torches
Lighted up the night's repose,
And from the flames like fabled Phoenix,
Our glorious liberty arose!

That old State House bell is silent,
Hushed is now its clamorous tongue;
But the spirit it awakened
Still is living — ever young;
And when we greet the smiling sunlight
On the fourth of each July,
We will ne'er forget the bellman
Who, betwixt the earth and sky,
Rang out loudly, "Independence";
Which, please God, shall never die!

★ 23 ★

Bunker Hill

MILLIONS of Americans have seen the famous Bunker Hill Monument in Boston, and many of them have thought of it as rising somehow by itself out of that battlefield. But such things as great monuments never merely happen. People have to plan them and build them and pay for them.

So it is necessary, if we are to understand this, to go back to the day when the Bunker Hill Monument was completed, and then back further still, to the years behind the scenes and to the people who made that day possible.

It was fifty years after the battle of Bunker Hill, on June 17, 1775, before the cornerstone of the monument was laid; and it was eighteen years more before the memorial was ready to be dedicated. That dedication took place on June 17, 1843.

What Daniel Webster, New England's most renowned orator, had to say at the ceremony belongs, of course, to our American Scriptures. But so does the story of how countless unnamed New England women had worked for years before he spoke. They are the story's silent heroines.

And it is pleasant to remember that Sara Josepha Hale, who organized and encouraged their efforts, is known to all of us by something else she did — whether or not we know she did it. For she was the author of "Mary Had a Little Lamb."

Bunker Hill

A Man

In reality sometimes, sometimes in dream,
Americans look down from that green hill
That rises over Boston, and with pride
Remember the June day when first our men,
Leaving their plows, their benches and their shops,
Stood firm for liberty against a foe
Well-trained and valiant. "Bunker Hill" —
The words are symbols of our nation's birth,
For here the spirit of our land took root
When we, whose lives knew only ways of peace,
Met the great test of battle unafraid
And gladly shed our blood in freedom's cause.
Yes, this is sacred ground and we have raised here
One great, up-reaching, everlasting sign
Of our devotion to our origins —
A granite needle stitching earth's green cover
To the blue canopy that lifts above.

A Woman

Just you hold your horses there, young fellow,
You've told the truth so far in pretty words
Maybe a mite too pretty for my taste,
New England as I am and plain-spoken.
That "granite needle", as you chose to call it,
Has quite a story when all's said and done.
Maybe you'd like to hear it. If you would,
Suppose you let me take you back through time
(New England women have been hanged for less,
But this one form of witching we do well)
And let us stand together looking up
On that straight shaft of polished stone
When it was new. The time, June seventeenth
In eighteen-forty-three. What do you behold?

MONUMENTS

A Man

A hundred thousand of our countrymen,
Marching through the streets of Boston toward us.
Already they crowd up the sunlit slope.

A Woman

And thirty bands are playing; count them, thirty.

A Man

There go the Massachusetts volunteers.

A Woman

And there the smart New Hampshire regiment,
And two more from the great state of New York.

A Man

The flag is everywhere — lining the streets,
Crowding the gay pavilion just above us
With multitudes of stars and countless bars —
Red, white, and blue, the colors shout in the sun.

A Woman

The time is near — it's early afternoon.
The President has entered the pavilion.

A Man

The people raise a joyful yell of greeting,
Now they cry, "Hurrah for good John Tyler!" —
Then suddenly are silent. Who are these?
These white-haired, bent, slow-stepping, gaunt old men,
Who falter up to the first row of seats
And stand, shading their eyes against the sun,
With wrinkled hands a-tremble now with age?

A Woman

These thirteen stood here once long years ago,
And they were young men bearing arms that day.
Their hands were smooth and brown, they did not tremble.
Let some old fellow tell you how it was —
You pick him out. Try Amos Farnsworth there:

Bunker Hill

We within the entrenchment and at a breastwork without, sustained the enemy's attack, killed and wounded great numbers, and repulsed them several times. And after bearing, for about two hours, as severe and heavy a fire as perhaps was known, and many having fired away all their ammunition . . . . we were overpowered by numbers. I did not leave the entrenchment until the enemy got in. I then retreated ten or fifteen rods. Then I received a wound in my right arm, the ball going thru a little below my elbow . . . . Another ball struck my back, taking off a piece of skin about as big as a penny . . . . Oh the goodness of God in preserving my life, altho they fell on my right hand and on my left!

A Woman
That is the story, told and told again
By every patriot throughout the land.
A Man
And this great obelisk now dares the clouds
To speak our gratitude to Amos Farnsworth
And all his comrades on that day of days.
A Woman
An obelisk you say? A monument
I call it, being Yankee, not Egyptian.
Bunker Hill Monument, lifting its head
To cloud and star, through sun and rain
Strong symbol of the changeless, loyal heart
And the unswerving, dauntless will to freedom.
A Man
You said there was a story?
A Woman

Yes, I did.
For this great shaft was twenty years abuilding.

205

MONUMENTS

I may as well be frank with you, young man.
It cost a lot more than we thought it would
When it was half-done or a little more,
Our money had been spent and there it stood. —
A dwarf — a crumbling ruin, struck to earth
Before it ever rose into the wind
That sweeps above this sacred hill of ours.
For years it stood there shaming us and then
A woman, editress of *Godey's Ladies' Book*,
Sara Josepha Hale, spoke for our women.
She sits below us — you can see her there —
And hear her, too, reading the words she wrote:

*

Impressed with the importance of this subject and thinking
the crisis one in which ladies may, without any infringement
of that feminine propriety which they should scrupulously
retain when coming before the public, offer their assistance—
we would seriously suggest that an attempt be made by the
women of Massachusetts (or of all New England, if that be
thought best) to raise by their own exertions the sum of
$50,000, to be appropriated to the finishing of the Bunker
Hill Monument.

A Man
We know the women's answer. Here it stands.
A Woman
Yes, here it stands, because New England wives —
Women of Salem, Worcester, Medford, Lynn,

Bunker Hill

Nantucket, Taunton and Jamaica Plain,
Northampton, Waltham, Beverly and Norwich
And many another neat old Yankee town —
Gave such a fair as never had been seen,
In Quincy Hall, here in the town of Boston;
A fair to sell the wares their hands had made —
Berthas and camisoles and hug-me-tights,
Confectioneries, pies and frosted cakes.
You see that granite column pierce the blue?
The myriad stitches of their tireless hands
Are in it. One block is embroidery,
And there's another that is all crochet.
This towering tribute to the man who fought
Does homage also to the waiting wife,
Alone in the doorway looking up the road,
Praying to see the loved one plodding home,
But ready for the age-old sacrifice,
Rather than see a people robbed of freedom.
Sara Josepha Hale, do tell us now,
Did you succeed? What came of the great fair?:

*

We can safely say that a sufficient sum has been received. It
is a source of gratification that so many of our own sex have
participated in this patriotic effort. It has shown what our
sex can do.

A Man
Now, look! Up there beside the speaker's platform,
Where people swarm like bees. Who is the man

207

Love and tears for the Blue
Tears and love for the Gray.

— FRANCIS MILES FINCH

PLATE THIRTY-THREE

UNION PRISONERS PLAYING BASEBALL, SALISBURY, NORTH CAROLINA, 1863

LITHOGRAPH AFTER DRAWING BY MAJOR OTTO BOTICHER. OWNED BY THE NEW-YORK HISTORICAL SOCIETY, NEW YORK CITY.

. . . these dead shall not have died in vain.

— ABRAHAM LINCOLN

PLATE THIRTY-FOUR

SQUARE AT GETTYSBURG

PHOTOGRAPHED BY M. B. BRADY. COURTESY OF THE LIBRARY OF CONGRESS, WASHINGTON, D. C.

210

The color of the ground was in him, the red earth.

— EDWIN MARKHAM

PLATE THIRTY-FIVE

THE PRESIDENT AND GENERAL McCLELLAN

PHOTOGRAPHED BY ALEX GARDNER AND PUBLISHED BY
M. B. BRADY. COURTESY OF THE LIBRARY OF CONGRESS,
WASHINGTON, D. C.

212

THE PRESIDENT AND GENERAL McCLELLAN

On the Battle-field of Antietam.

213

Here, coffin that slowly passes
I give you my sprig of lilac.

—WALT WHITMAN

PLATE THIRTY-SIX

FUNERAL PROCESSION OF
ABRAHAM LINCOLN PASSING THROUGH
CITY HALL PARK, NEW YORK CITY

COURTESY OF THE BLAND GALLERY, NEW YORK CITY.

215

. . . *let the annual return of this day forever refresh our recollection of these rights.*

—Thomas Jefferson

PLATE THIRTY-SEVEN

THE DAY WE CELEBRATE, FOURTH OF JULY

ENGRAVING BY JOHN C. MCRAE, 1875, OWNED BY THE NEW-YORK HISTORICAL SOCIETY, NEW YORK CITY.

216

217

. . . true Americanism comprehends the noblest ideas that ever swell a human heart with pride.

— CARL SCHURZ

PLATE THIRTY-EIGHT

NEW ENGLAND COUNTRY SCHOOL

PAINTED BY WINSLOW HOMER, FROM THE COLLECTION OF ADDISON GALLERY OF AMERICAN ART, PHILLIPS ACADEMY, ANDOVER, MASSACHUSETTS.

219

Providence has showered on this favorite land blessings without number, and has chosen you, as the guardians of freedom, to preserve it.

—ANDREW JACKSON

PLATE THIRTY-NINE

INTERIOR OF A BUTCHER SHOP

PAINTED ATTRIBUTED TO WILLIAM S. MOUNT (ATTRIBUTION DOUBTFUL). COURTESY OF THE NEWARK MUSEUM, NEWARK, NEW JERSEY.

221

To Him upon the threshold of new life
We raise our hymn of deep thanksgiving.

PLATE FORTY

THANKSGIVING DAY . . . THE DINNER

ILLUSTRATION BY WINSLOW HOMER IN HARPER'S WEEKLY, NOVEMBER 27, 1858. COURTESY OF THE METROPOLITAN MUSEUM OF ART, NEW YORK CITY.

222

223

Bunker Hill

Who climbs the steps? Where have I seen that face —
The wide and thoughtful brow — the deep-set eyes?
         A Woman
Now you shall hear what no man of your time
Has ever heard: the deep impassioned voice
That rolls in thunder, words like organ notes,
Sounding above us. This is Daniel Webster —
Speaking for the land as few before or since:

        ★

The Bunker Hill Monument is finished. Here it stands . . . .
It is itself the orator of this occasion . . . .The powerful
speaker stands motionless before us . . . . Today it speaks to
us . . . . Its speech will be of patriotism and courage; of civil
and religious liberty; of free government; . . . . and of the
immortal memory of those who, with heroic devotion, have
sacrificed their lives for their country . . . .

If there was nothing of value in the principles of the
American Revolution, then there is nothing valuable in the
battle of Bunker Hill and its consequences. But if the Revolution was an era . . . . (in the history of man) favorable to
human happiness, if it was an event which marked the progress of man all over the world from despotism to liberty,
then this monument is not raised without cause . . . .

. . . . Let us hold fast the great truth, that communities are
responsible, as well as individuals; that no government is
respectable, which is not just; that without unspotted purity
of public faith, ... no mere forms of government, no
machinery of laws can give dignity to political society . . . .

And then, when honored and decrepit age shall lean against

the base of this monument, and troops of ingenuous youth shall be gathered round it, and when the one shall speak to the other of its objects, ... there shall rise from every youthful breast the ejaculation, "Thank God, I — I also — AM AN AMERICAN!

PRINCIPLES

The Bill of Rights

THE first ten Amendments to the Constitution of the United States are known as the American Bill of Rights.

These ten amendments were adopted by the first Congress of the United States in 1789. Later amendments came so slowly, one by one, that it was 142 years before another ten had been adopted and ratified. But the first ten came at once in response to the will of the whole people.

For the people were determined that if they were to begin life under a new constitution, it must at the very outset guarantee them their rights.

Of course the people did not think of these as new rights. They were the old rights, as old as English liberty, under which Americans had lived while they were still colonies of the British Empire. Our people had taken up arms to defend those rights, which they thought were threatened by the imperial government.

Then came the proposed Constitution of the United States. As proposed, it seemed to many Americans to pay too much attention to the powers of the government, and too little to the rights of the people.

Well, Americans who had rebelled against one government in defense of their ancient rights, had no intention of giving up those rights under the new government even if they had set it up themselves. So the American people demanded that a Bill of Rights be incorporated in the Constitution.

Those people remembered the fierce desire for freedom of worship that had brought Pilgrims and Puritans to New England, and Quakers to Pennsylvania, and Catholics to Maryland; the triumphant fight for a free press in the colony of New York; the freedoms of speech and assembly and petition which the Americans had won by long struggle and were determined to hold on to. And the Bill of Rights put those memories into law:

★

Article 1. . . . . Congress shall make no law respecting an establishment of religion, or prohibiting the free exercise thereof; or abridging the freedom of speech, or of the press; or the right of people peaceably to assemble, and to petition the government for a redress of grievances.

The first step of a despotic government is to disarm the people. The Americans of 1789 did not intend to be disarmed. Family by family, settlement by settlement, they had defended themselves against the Indians. Many of them got their food or part of it by hunting. Many of the battles of the revolution had been fought by men with their own muskets or rifles in their hands. So now:

PRINCIPLES

*

Article 2. . . . . A well regulated Militia, being necessary to the security of a free State, the right of the people to keep and bear Arms, shall not be infringed.

Before the Revolution many Americans had been forced, whether they liked it or not, to furnish quarters, in their own houses, for soldiers who had come to suppress them. There was to be no more of that:

*

Article 3. . . . . No Soldier shall, in time of peace be quartered in any house, without the consent of the Owner, nor in time of war, but in a manner to be prescribed by law.

Nor should the new government have any more right than the old to arrest the people, or to invade their houses, except for lawful cause and in a lawful way. No secret police for the Americans:

*

Article 4. . . . . The right of the people to be secure in their persons, houses, papers, and effects, against unreasonable searches and seizures, shall not be violated, and no Warrants shall issue, but upon probable cause, supported by Oath or

230

The Bill of Rights

affirmation, and particularly describing the place to be searched, and the persons or things to be seized.

Life, liberty, and property were still to be secure against unjust acts, deliberate or ignorant, of government or courts. Accused men must continue to have rights till they were found guilty:

★

Article 5. . . . . No person shall be held to answer for a capital, or otherwise infamous crime, unless on a presentment or indictment of a Grand Jury, except in cases arising in the land or naval forces, or in the Militia, when in actual service in time of War or public danger; nor shall any person be subject for the same offense to be twice put in jeopardy of life or limb; nor shall he compelled in any criminal case to be a witness against himself, nor be deprived of life, liberty, or property, without due process of law; nor shall private property be taken for public use, without just compensation.

The ancient right of trial by jury, either in criminal or civil cases, must be maintained, for without this right, there would be no rights at all. Articles 6 and 7 guarantee the right of trial by jury in detail.

★

Article 6. . . . . In all criminal prosecutions, the accused shall enjoy the right to a speedy and public trial, by an impartial

★ 25 ★

Freedom of the Press

THERE is one American freedom in particular which is in our very bones. It is the freedom of speaking and printing. When a man asks, "This is a free country, isn't it?" we know he means to speak his mind, and we give him a chance, and then answer him.

Think how we should have felt if we had fought in the dark during the recent war, with no radio and press to bring us all the news that it was safe to make known. True news is never so bad as no news would be. Fear and worry rise like a black cloud over ignorance. The truth makes us free.

One of the rights Americans have guarded most zealously through the years is that of telling people what we think in print. Let your imagination take you back through the years to a little, hot printing-house in the town of Boston in June of the year 1722.

A boy of seventeen is trying to get out a newspaper. The title at the top of the sheet reads *The New England Courant.* His older brother, owner of the paper, has been put in jail, for printing criticism of governmental authorities. The boy knows that he himself may go to prison for the words he is printing — yet he does not hesitate.

★

Without freedom of thought there can be no such thing as

wisdom — and no such thing as public liberty without freedom of speech.

That the words were not his own but a quotation from the *London Journal* did not lessen the force of the argument of the boy printer, Benjamin Franklin. But an obstinate government across the sea continued to suppress the printing of critical comment in the American colonies. Arrogant governors influenced the King of England, George II, to prohibit freedom of the press in the great province of New York:

★

Forasmuch as great inconvenience may arise by the liberty of printing within our province of New York, you are to provide that no person keep any press . . . . nor that any book, pamphlet or other matters whatsoever be printed without your especial leave and license be first obtained.

Nevertheless, enemies of Governor Cosby's dictator-like rule in old New York started a newspaper — the *Weekly Journal* — and chose as editor John Peter Zenger, immigrant from the banks of the Rhine. Zenger set about printing strong criticism of the governor and was arrested and thrown into jail. Then Governor Cosby really went to work to assure the prisoner's conviction on charges of libel. He had the two lawyers who dared to represent Zenger disbarred for challenging the jurisdiction of the court. And he kept Zenger in jail for nine months. But the dauntless printer kept on editing the *Weekly Journal*. Each day his wife came to the prison and John Peter Zenger told her — through a hole in the door of his cell — what he wanted published in the next issue:

★

It is the great design of this paper to maintain and explain the glorious principles of Liberty and to expose the art of those who would darken or destroy them.

John Peter Zenger was tried in midsummer in the old City Hall. It stood on Wall Street where the Sub-Treasury Building now stands. The attorney-general, a favorite of the Governor's little court, denounced the editor bitterly and the Governor's judge nodded his head in agreement.

The cause of freedom of the press seemed hopelessly lost when the time came for the defense to present its case. Then the courtroom audience gasped. An old man had risen. He was Andrew Hamilton — the finest lawyer in all the colonies. Though his body was weak with years he had come all the way from Philadelphia to speak for the rights of John Peter Zenger and the rights of all men:

★

It is a privilege — I will go farther, it is a right which all free men claim, to complain when they are hurt; they have

Freedom of the Press

a right publicly to remonstrate against abuses of power . . . . to put their neighbors upon their guard against craft or open violence of men in authority, and to assert with courage the sense they have of the blessings of liberty — and their reso- lution at all hazards to preserve it. Men who injure and oppress the people under their administration provoke them to cry out and complain, and then make that very complaint the foundation for new oppressions.

The question before the court and you, gentlemen of the jury, is not of small and private concern; it is not the cause of a poor printer, nor of New York alone, which we are try- ing. No! . . . . It is the best cause, it is the cause of liberty!

When the old man stopped speaking, there was stillness in the hot courtroom. Slowly the jury filed out and the crowd, knowing every one of them — for New York was a little city then — felt that they were trustworthy men who would give an honest verdict. There was a long wait. The sultry August day moved slowly toward its close. Then — there was the jury marching back again. Their foreman spoke out for all people everywhere who love freedom and hate tyranny:

★

We find the defendant, John Peter Zenger, not guilty!

There was no silence after that speech. The crowd's yell shook the courtroom. While the enraged judge fumed and

237

spluttered, the waiting people outside in Wall Street took up the exulting cry. It spread over the city like a blowing flame — the flame of freedom. New York rejoiced that it had won a round in the everlasting conflict men must wage to keep their civil rights.

Andrew Hamilton, being a wise man, knew that there would be other battles like this — in New York, in Boston, in his own city of Philadelphia — but he had fought a good fight and he had won it.

But there was one great and glorious fact that he could not know. It was that, through battles such as his own, and those that had gone before in this land which he loved, a new nation would be born — a nation whose very foundations would rest on human rights. Benjamin Franklin and Andrew Hamilton had fought for the same thing — and it was because they kept the love of freedom alive here in this country that eventually that part of our constitution known as the Bill of Rights was born. Old Andrew Hamilton did not know it, but his courageous fight helped make it possible that more than half a century later, the very first session of our Congress wrote into our Constitution one of its most sacred scriptures. Hear the voice of James Madison reading to that Congress the words which have become our precious heritage:

*

Congress shall make no law respecting an establishment of religion, or prohibiting the free exercise thereof, or abridging the freedom of speech, or of the press, or the right of the people peaceably to assemble, and to petition the government for a redress of grievances.

★ 26 ★

Carl Schurz on True Americanism

IN FANEUIL HALL, in Boston, a memorable speech was delivered on the evening of April 18, 1859. To this spacious room the people of Boston had come together to debate the issues of the Revolution. Here they had taken the steps that gave Faneuil Hall its other name: The Cradle of Liberty.

The room was packed with nearly two thousand men, besides the women in the galleries. They had come together that night to listen — in the heart of New England — to a speaker from Wisconsin, a man who was born in Germany and who had been a naturalized American citizen for only two years. His name was Carl Schurz, and he was to speak on True Americanism.

Schurz had been invited to Boston by a group of serious young men, who were troubled over the rise of a new political party. It called itself the American Party — but it was in fact a secret organization.

When you asked one of its members about it, he said he knew nothing. So other people called them the Know-Nothings. Of course, the Know-Nothings did not last. No party based on prejudice has ever lasted long in the United States. But that night, in Faneuil Hall, there were many people who were deeply worried about these Know-Nothings.

They were natives, and they disliked foreign-born Americans. They claimed to be the only real Americans. They aimed, so far as possible, to keep America for Americans like themselves.

The serious, troubled young men who had invited Carl Schurz to come from the Middle West to speak in Boston were themselves native Protestant Anglo-Saxon Americans. But they knew that the so-called native American stocks are descended from settlers of many nationalities. Come to think about it, Peter Faneuil, who gave Boston this Hall, and Paul Revere, whose ride started on this night of the year in 1775, were both sons of men who came to America from France.

Carl Schurz, the "foreigner" who was soon to speak, when he was a schoolboy on the Rhine found his first great hero in George Washington. As a student at a German university, Schurz believed in the United States as the ideal to which all free men should look. At twenty he fought the Prussians in a short and unsuccessful revolution, and was driven into exile. At twenty-three he came to the United States. This was in 1852. Lately he had been campaigning for Abraham Lincoln in the Middle West, and this young immigrant was later to be a general in the Union Army, a member of a President's Cabinet, and the ambassador of the United States to Spain.

He was not a native American. But he was a natural American. He talked as if the older America were again fresh and new in him. And the Bostonians who had invited him believed that Carl Schurz, born in a foreign country, would be at home in Faneuil Hall.

So that evening in April, 1859, Schurz is being introduced to a Boston audience. He stepped forward and began to speak:

*

No man that loves liberty, wherever he may first have seen the light of day, can fail on this sacred spot to pay his tribute to Americanism. And here, with all these glorious memories crowding upon my heart, I will offer mine. I, born in a foreign land, pay my tribute to Americanism. Yes. For to me the word Americanism, true Americanism, comprehends the noblest ideas that ever swelled a human heart with pride.

You may tell me that these views are visionary, that the destiny of this country is less exalted, that the American people are less great than I think they are or ought to be. I answer, ideals are like stars; you will not succeed in touching them with your hands. . . .

Every people, every creed, every class of society has contributed its share to that wonderful mixture out of which is to grow the great nation of the new world. It is true, the Anglo-Saxon establishes and maintains his supremacy, but without wholly absorbing the other national elements. They modify each other, and their peculiar characteristics are to be blended together by the all-assimilating power of freedom. This is the origin of the American nationality, which did not spring from one family, one tribe, one country, but incorporates the vigorous elements of all civilized nations on earth. . . .

We see the vigorous elements of all nations — peacefully congregating and mingling together on virgin soil . . . . undertaking to commence a new era in the history of the world, without first destroying the results of the progress of past periods; undertaking to found a new, cosmopolitan nation, without marching over the dead bodies of slain millions.

Thus was founded the great colony of free humanity, which has not Old England alone, but the *world*, for its mother country.

In this colony of free humanity, they established the Republic of Equal Rights, where the title of manhood is the title to citizenship. . . . This was the dream of the truest friends of man from the beginning. For this the noblest blood of martyrs has been shed. For this, mankind has waded through seas of blood and tears.

From the equality of rights springs the identity of the highest interests. You cannot subvert your neighbor's rights without striking a dangerous blow at your own. And when the rights of one cannot be infringed without finding a ready defense in all others, who defend their own rights in defending his, then and only then, are the rights of all safe. . . .

Equality of rights, embodied in general self-government, is the great moral element in modern democracy. . . . There is the solid foundation of our system of government. There is our greatness. There is our safety. There, and nowhere else! . . . .

This is true Americanism. And to this I pay the tribute of my devotion.

Those are the words of Carl Schurz on true Americanism.

In the American Scriptures there is nowhere a finer description of what America has been, and must go on being, than this:

Carl Schurz on True Americanism

".... the great colony of free humanity, which has the world for its mother country."

The idea which Carl Schurz here expressed was too strong for the Know-Nothings, who, as a party, soon disappeared from American political life. And Americans since that time have had more and more reason to believe that the world is indeed the mother country of America.

If anybody doubts that this is still true, let him look at any list of American soldiers or sailors, marines or flyers, reported killed or wounded or missing in the war we lately waged to defend all that Americans hold dear. In their names, brought together in one brotherhood from all the nations and languages of the earth, he will find the answer.

★ 27 ★

Crusade for Freedom ·

I N THE autumn of 1943, while Americans were offering their lives on battlefronts throughout the world in the unending crusade for freedom, the Congress of the United States looked ahead to the time when actual fighting would be ended. It pledged itself to establish "a general international organization, based on the principle of the sovereign equality of all peace-loving states for the maintenance of international peace and security."

Twenty-four years before, in 1919, President Woodrow Wilson in his last public speech had prophesied the eventual triumph of these ideals.

They were the same ideals he had expressed in his famous war message to Congress, on April 2, 1917. Here is a part of that message:

★

We are now about to accept gage of battle with this natural foe to liberty and shall, if necessary, spend the whole force of the Nation to check and nullify its pretensions and its power. We are glad . . . . to fight thus for the ultimate peace of the world and for the liberation of its peoples, the German peoples included: for the rights of nations great and small and the privilege of men everywhere to choose their way of life and of obedience. The world must be made safe for democracy. Its peace must be planted upon the tested foundations of political liberty. We have no selfish ends to serve. We desire no conquest, no dominion. We seek no indemnities for ourselves, no material compensation for the sacrifices we shall freely make. We are but one of the champions of the rights of mankind. We shall be satisfied when those rights have been made as secure as the faith and the freedom of the nations can make them. ...

.... There are, it may be, many months of fiery trial and sacrifice ahead of us. It is a fearful thing to lead this great peaceful people into war, into the most terrible and disastrous of all wars, civilization itself seeming to be in the balance. But the right is more precious than peace, and we shall fight for the things which we have always carried nearest our hearts, — for democracy, for the right of those who submit to authority to have a voice in their own Governments, for the rights and liberties of small nations, for a universal dominion of right by such a concert of free peoples as shall bring peace and safety to all nations and make the world itself at last free. To such a task we can dedicate our lives and our fortunes, everything that we are and everything that we have, with the pride of those who know that the day has come when America is privileged to spend her blood and her might for the principles that gave her birth and happiness and the peace which she has treasured. God helping her, she can do no other.

And here is a part of the prophetic speech delivered by Woodrow Wilson at Pueblo, Colorado, in September, 1919. It was his last address as President. He was already a sick man. Those who heard him noticed the grayness of his face, and the twitching of one cheek. With the clear vision of one already close to death, he foresaw that if he failed in his mission, America would once more, and within a generation, be compelled to send "men who love liberty enough to leave their homes and fight for it" to distant fields of battle:

*

What of our pledges to the men that lie dead in France? We said that they went over there not to prove the prowess of America or her readiness for another war but to see to it that there never was such a war again. . . . I think of my clients in this case. My clients are the children; my clients are the next generation. They do not know what promises and bonds I undertook when I ordered the armies of the United States to the soil of France, but I know, and I intend to redeem my pledges to the children; . . . .

Again and again, my fellow citizens, mothers who lost their sons in France have come to me and, taking my hand, have shed tears upon it not only, but they have added, "God Bless You, Mr. President!" . . . . I ordered their sons oversea. I consented to their sons being put in the most difficult parts of the battle line, where death was certain. . . . Why should they weep upon my hand and call down the blessings of God upon me? Because they believe that their boys died for something that vastly transcends any of the immediate and palpable objects of the war. They believe, and they rightly believe, that their sons saved the liberty of the world. They believed that wrapped up with the liberty of the world is the continuous protection of that liberty by the concerted powers of all civilized people. They believe that this sacrifice was made in order that other sons should not be called upon for a similar gift — the gift of life, the gift of all that died — .... These men were crusaders. They were going forth to prove the might of justice and right, and all the world accepted them as crusaders, ... not only those boys who came home, but those dear ghosts that still deploy upon the fields of France. ...

The arrangements of justice do not stand of themselves, my fellow citizens .... they need the support of the combined power of the great nations of the world .... I believe that men will see the truth, eye to eye and face to face. There is one thing that the American people always rise to and extend their hand to, and that is the truth of justice and of liberty and of peace. We have accepted that truth and we are going to be led by it, and it is going to lead us, and through us the world, out into pastures of quietness and peace such as the world never dreamed of before.

THE WEST

Lewis and Clark

L ET me recall for you the history of a small group of forty-five American soldiers engaged in one of the most courageous enterprises of our history. The time is over a hundred and forty years ago. The shadow of a conqueror had stretched across Europe and put the United States in peril. He was Napoleon. Later we were to fight a war because of him. But now his greatest threat to us had ended. For the danger that our little nation, only fifteen years old, would break apart along the line of the Alleghany Mountains or be crushed by Napoleon's North American empire — that danger had vanished when the President, Thomas Jefferson, sent envoys to buy the mouth of the Mississippi River from France. They had hoped to buy the island of New Orleans. They had ended by buying Louisiana.

They had bought for us, that is, all the lands north of Texas and westward from the Mississippi to the crest of those Rocky Mountains which no American had ever seen. They had bought an untravelled wilderness which we now call Arkansas, Missouri, Iowa, Nebraska, North and South Dakota, nearly all of Oklahoma, Kansas, Wyoming and Montana, most of Minnesota, and part of Colorado. All but an edge of this immensity was unknown. Thomas Jefferson had resolved to make the unknown known. To bring Louisiana out of myth and conjecture.

Lewis and Clark

So he had ordered these forty-five soldiers to ascend the Missouri River from St. Louis, to cross the Rocky Mountains, and to find a great river whose mouth a Boston sea captain had entered twelve years before, a river named for his ship, *Columbia.* They were led by Captain Meriwether Lewis and Captain William Clark. Let us glance at them on Christmas Day of 1804.

They were seven months out of St. Louis, sixteen hundred miles up the Missouri River. Here, sixty miles northward from the site of Bismarck, North Dakota, near a village of the friendly Mandan Indians, they had halted for the winter and built a triangular fort of logs. The river was frozen and big herds of buffalo were crossing the ice.

The captains had told the Mandans that Christmas was the Great Medicine Day of the whites. The only Indians who saw the celebration were three squaws, the wives of a Canadian who had been hired as an interpreter, one of whom was the immortal Sacajawea. Sacajawea, then, heard the three volleys of musketry that greeted the Christmas sun and shared the dinner of buffalo meat, to which the captains added a holiday ration of flour, dried fruit, and pepper, and three cups of rum apiece.

She watched the games on the frozen snow and at night saw these white men dance their jigs and hoedowns, while one played a fiddle and all sang the songs which a century and a half have made nostalgic in our ears. This to the crimson of great fires in the log fort, while northern lights were mirrored in the snow and the winds of the high plains howled overhead.

Thus we must see them all winter long. By day they hunted, improved their fort, made axes for the Indians or treated their illnesses or watched their ceremonies. But by night, before those fires, Lewis and Clark gathered the chiefs round them and summoned warriors who had ventured westward. For a few miles beyond this rude fort the unknown West began. None knew what it contained but all knew its dangers were manifold and constant, not least of them Indians more formidable than the genial Mandans — Indians such as the Sioux, whom the captains had already to defy, the Assiniboins, the implacable Blackfeet. And somewhere near the Rockies, they hoped to meet the Shoshones, from whom Sacajawea had been stolen when a little girl. If the Shoshones proved friendly, if they would sell food and horses, then it was possible to hope that these venturers might complete their journey.

But how did the unmapped rivers come down? How did the mountain ranges lie? Where were there passes? Where trails? Where falls or rapids? Where deserts?

The firelight shines on copper faces. The chiefs sprinkle sand to represent mountains. They scrawl river courses in it with a finger tip. They repeat the dim rumors they have heard, numbering camps or moons with little twigs. The captains listen. For they are the mind of civilized men at the boundary of knowledge. They are the United States moving toward its destiny.

The snows end, the air gentles, the ice breaks up, the whistling swans come northward. Lewis and Clark get the boats into the river. They dispatch a final letter to Thomas

Lewis and Clark

Jefferson in Washington, reduce their party to thirty-two, and start west. Day by day novelty and strangeness increase around them; the badlands, the sagebrush, the alkali, the unnamed plants, the grizzly bears and mountain sheep which no white man before them had described.

A moment's lapse of vigilance, a single stupidity, one failure to interpret aright the alien strangeness they are traveling, and all of them — soldiers, captains, Sacajawea and the infant son she carries strapped to her back — would be snuffed out by the impersonal hostility of the wilderness.

Past the Yellowstone River and the long list of rivers they named: the Big Muddy, the Milk, the Musselshell, Maria's River. A blue haze darkens the horizon — the Rocky Mountains are in sight. The spray from the Great Falls of the Missouri is blown for the first time against white men's cheeks. On to the Three Forks of the Missouri, and up the one they name the Jefferson.

They abandon their boats and with agonizing labor reach the foot of the Continental Divide. Here they meet the Shoshones and the chief proves to be the elder brother of Sacajawea, from whose lodge she was stolen as a child. So at the crisis of the expedition, with success or utter failure hanging poised, the Indian woman saves them all, not for the first nor for the last time.

The Shoshones sell them horses and a little food. But now they have reached the limit of human strength, and as they toil over range after range of mountains, fevers and fluxes assail them and starvation draws near. But they come down to gentler country, where their health improves and they build dugout canoes. They launch into the Kooskooskee River, go down it to the Snake, and at last reach the Columbia. So down its widening waters, till one triumphant day Clark may write in his journal, "ocean in view," and for the first time Americans traveling overland have reached the Pacific.

They build another fort, and on a large pine tree Clark carves a legend: "William Clark, December 3, 1805. By land from the United States in 1804 and 5."

And so it was, against all probability, against wilderness, Indians, and the hourly hazard of death — by land from the United States. The Americans had crossed their continent. The Northwest Passage, for which the Old World searched in vain through three centuries, had been achieved.

There we may leave them as their second Christmas comes on, looking across the Pacific toward China, the Indies, and Japan. But the wilderness behind them has a trail blazed across it. Today the whistle of freight trains echoes across the grass that bent to their footsteps, and the canyons they toiled through hear the engines of planes making their passage in hours where they took months. The United States has filled the wilderness they broke with the cities and dams, the factories and mines, the orchards and wheat fields of the living West. Where they led, we have followed.

★ 29 ★

The Alamo

TEXAS, the Lone Star State, was for several years an independent republic, not yet a part of the United States. It won its independence from Mexico in a short, fierce war in 1836. Many Americans have forgotten about that little war—but not about the famous siege of the Alamo which ended in March of that year.

A Mexican army, under General Santa Anna, had come to San Antonio to put down the Texas revolution. A detachment of Texas soldiers, commanded by Colonel William Barret Travis, and a band of volunteers led by Colonel James Bowie, established themselves in the old Alamo mission that now served them as a fort. With them was Colonel David Crockett of Tennessee, who had come to Texas to take up the cause of men fighting for their liberty. There were less than two hundred Texans all told in the Alamo, and at least ten times that many men in the besieging forces.

Not one of the Texans who fought there lived to tell the story. But some of Travis's valiant words have been preserved, and some other words so like Crockett's that they may be his. Round these words, and round the deeds of the defenders of the Alamo, one of America's most gallant stories has grown up.

Neither snow nor rain nor heat nor gloom of night stays these
couriers from the swift completion of their appointed rounds.

PLATE FORTY-ONE

THE OVERLAND PONY EXPRESS

FROM A PAINTING BY GEORGE M. OTTINGER FOR HARPER'S WEEKLY, NOVEMBER 2, 1867.
COURTESY OF THE NEW YORK PUBLIC LIBRARY, NEW YORK CITY.

THE OVERLAND PONY EXPRESS.—[Photographed by Savage, Salt Lake City, from a Painting by George M. Ottinger.]

Let us make the iron road, and make it from sea to sea.

—Thomas Hart Benton

THE FIRST TRANSCONTINENTAL TRAIN LEAVING SACRAMENTO

PAINTED BY JOSEPH BECKER. COURTESY OF MRS. HARRY MACNEILL BLAND.

258

259

What is a flag? . . . It is the wagons and the men on foot going westward.

— Flag Day, 1940

PLATE FORTY-THREE

THE EMIGRANTS

PAINTED BY FREDERICK REMINGTON. COURTESY OF THE MUSEUM OF FINE ARTS, HOUSTON, TEXAS. FROM THE COLLECTION GIVEN BY THE HOGG BROTHERS TO THE MUSEUM.

260

261

These are flesh of our flesh, bone of our bone, blood of our blood,
a lasting part of what we are.

— FLAG DAY, 1940

PLATE FORTY-FOUR

COWBOYS COMING TO TOWN

PAINTED BY FREDERICK REMINGTON. COURTESY OF THE NEW YORK PUBLIC LIBRARY, NEW YORK CITY.

262

What is a flag? ... It is a great multitude of people on pilgrimage ... filled with such a hope as never caught the imagination and the hearts of any nation on earth before.

— FLAG DAY, 1940

PLATE FORTY-FIVE

AT THE FAIR GROUNDS

CURRIER AND IVES PRINT. FROM THE MABEL BRADY GARVAN COLLECTION. COURTESY OF YALE UNIVERSITY ART GALLERY, NEW HAVEN, CONNECTICUT.

. . . the great colony of free humanity which has the world for its mother country.

— CARL SCHURZ

PLATE FORTY-SIX

IN THE LAND OF PROMISE

PAINTED BY CHARLES FREDERICK ULRICH. FROM THE PERMANENT COLLECTION OF THE CORCORAN GALLERY OF ART, WASHINGTON, D. C.

. . . communities are responsible as well as individuals . . . no government is responsible which is not just.

—DANIEL WEBSTER

PLATE FORTY-SEVEN

THE LONGSHOREMAN'S NOON

PAINTED BY JOHN GEORGE BROWN. FROM THE PERMANENT COLLECTION OF THE
CORCORAN GALLERY OF ART, WASHINGTON, D. C.

268

269

Whenever even justice is assailed
Strong men will rise, as in the years gone by.

The Alamo

No words can tell this tale. Our tongues are stilled.
Whenever we behold the thick-walled mission,
Standing near San Antonio's winding stream.
Only the heart can speak its silent homage,
Remembering the grove of cotton-woods,
The crumbling, roofless church inside the walls
And valiant men, tall breakers of the cane,
Wild riders of the swelling western waters,
Kentucky's hunters, sons of Tennessee,
Who gave their lives for freedom's sake in Texas
Within the conquered walls of the Alamo.
Millions of stars made bright the deep dark sky
When Santa Anna's army reached the river
And halted there. Then slow the sunrise came,
Flooding the plain with level, golden light.
Long shadows of the foe's great cannon fell
Across the land, black harbingers of death,
While Colonel William Travis wrote a letter:

*

Commandancy of the Alamo, Texas,
February 24, 1836.—
To the people of Texas and all Americans in the world.
Fellow citizens and compatriots: I am besieged by a thousand
or more of the Mexicans under Santa Anna. I have sustained
a continual bombardment and cannonade for twenty-four
hours and have not lost a man. The enemy has demanded a
surrender at discretion; otherwise the garrison are to be put
to the sword if the fort is taken. I have answered the demand
with a cannon shot, and our flag still waves proudly from the
walls. *I shall never surrender nor retreat.* Then, I call on

273

you in the name of liberty, of patriotism, and everything
dear to the American character, to come to our aid with all
dispatch. The enemy is receiving reinforcements daily and
will no doubt increase to three or four thousand in four or
five days. If this call is neglected, I am determined to sustain
myself as long as possible and die like a soldier who never
forgets what is due to his own honor and that of his country.
VICTORY OR DEATH.

> William Barret Travis
> Lieutenant Colonel, Commandant

Six days went by. The host beside the stream
Grew larger, darkening the far-spread land.
In the Alamo a hundred and fifty men
Stood to their guns and waited out the hours,
Praying that somehow help would come to them.
Then shadows flitted from the star-filled river
And thirty-two armed men from old Gonzales
Stood at the gates of the surrounded fort,
Asking to perish rather than to live
And know that others died and they not there.
Day came and on the walls crouched the defenders,
Among them lank Jim Bowie, who had struck
His hilted knife to many an evil heart,
And Davy Crockett, nursed on panther's milk —
Or so he said — who hung his powder-horn
Upon the gleaming hook of the new moon;
Crockett, the canebrake coonskin congressman,
The yellow blossom of the forest aisles,
Writing away the last dear hours of life,
Telling their story in his homely words,
Words that proclaim the birth of mighty Texas:

The Alamo

*

March the first — The enemy's forces have been increasing
in numbers daily, notwithstanding they have lost about 300
men in the several assaults they have made upon us. Colonel
Bowie's illness still continues, but he manages to crawl from
his bed every day, that his comrades may see him. His presence alone is a tower of strength. The enemy becomes more
daring as his numbers increase.

March the second — This day the delegates meet in general convention at the town of Washington to frame our
Declaration of Independence. That the sacred instrument
may never be trampled on by the children of those who have
freely shed their blood to establish it is the sincere wish of
Davy Crockett.

March the 4th — Pop, pop, pop! Bom, bom, bom!
throughout the day. No time for memorandums now. Go
ahead! Liberty and independence forever!

The foe has raised the red flag of no quarter.
His bugles sound the call of fire and blood.
The Americans watch the sun go down and know
Their eyes will see it rise but once again.
Bill Travis, struck with fever, from his cot
Calls to his men at midnight. Torches flare
Before the altar of the mission church,
Filling the aisles with intermittent light,
Striking grim faces with a sudden gleam.
The sick man lifts his tired head and speaks:

*

We are overwhelmed and our fate is sealed. Within a few
days, perhaps within a few hours, we must be in eternity. It

is no longer a question of how we may save our lives, but how best to prepare for death and serve our country. If we surrender we shall be shot without taking the life of a single one of our enemy. If we try to make our escape, we shall be butchered before we can dispatch our adversaries. To either of these courses I am opposed and I ask you to withstand the advance of the enemy. When they shall storm the fort and scale our walls at last, let us slay them as they come. As they leap over the ramparts, slay we all of them, until our arms are powerless to lift our swords in defense of ourselves, our comrades, our country. Yet to every man I give permission to surrender or attempt to escape. My desire and decision is to remain in the fort and fight as long as breath remains in my body. Do as you think best, each of you. Those who consent to remain with me to the end will give me joy unspeakable.

The end comes swiftly when the morning breaks
Across the plain. Drums beat and bugles call,
And all the enemy's five thousand men
Begin the charge. They drop in lifeless windrows,
But ever they come on, relentless waves
That must inevitably reach the shore.
The battering rams beat like giant drums
Upon the stout old gates until they yield,
And the foe floods in as freshets flow in spring
Back in Kentucky and in Tennessee.
The Americans fight their way down to the church
And there before the altar pile the slain
In one great human rampart. There they stand,
Their ammunition gone, but still they slash
And jab and strike until the last one falls

The Alamo

— And sudden stillness settles over all.
The enemy has won the Alamo
And all of its hundred and eighty-two
Have met swift death within its conquered walls.
Only a woman and her baby live
Of all Americans within the mission.
Wounded, but holding close the tiny child,
Sue Dickerson related her tragic story:

*

The struggle lasted more than two hours when my husband
rushed into the church where I was with my child and ex-
claimed, "They are inside our walls. All is lost. If they spare
you, save my child!" Then, with a parting kiss, he drew his
sword and plunged into the strife.

When dusk had drifted through the Alamo,
The foemen brought in wood from out the forest
And made a towering pile in which they placed
The bodies of our heroes. Then the stars
Came out and flames licked upward toward them.
And so these men of the woods and winds and streams
Went back into the elements they loved,
And we who honor them, can feel them there.
They are our brave. They speak in every breath
That blows above America. They say
Strong words of comfort to us while their breed,
Sons of their spirit, hold the Alamo
That is the blessed land we trust and love:

THE WEST

"Thermopylae had her messenger of defeat;
The Alamo had none." For we who fight
For justice to all men, a world made free,
Count life well lost in this our glorious cause.

★ 30 ★

The Pony Express

MAN, let us now and then remember, is the only animal that has a history and knows he has one, and that makes some use of his history in shaping his conduct and planning his future. Man does not live by instinct alone but looks before and after, remembering, reasoning and hoping.

To move through American history is to renew our fellowship with many men and women who, at different times, have been links, whether they fully knew it or not, in the great chain of our nation's life.

Few things now matter more to us than the coming and going of letters between us and our loved ones. Few things in the whole history of the United States have ever been so magnificent as the immense and incredible services which our Post Office has performed for the American people.

After all, the American Post Office was first organized by Benjamin Franklin, the first American of world renown. It was the captains of American ships who first learned how to hasten their voyages westward across the Atlantic by avoiding the Gulf Stream, and so expedited the American mails. It was an American, John Jeffries, of Boston who, as long ago as January, 1785, carried the first letters ever to go by air in the balloon flight he made with Pierre Blanchard in that month across the English Channel. And the plains of the American West saw the valiant chapter of mail-carrying which is known as the Pony Express.

The year was 1860 and spring had come to the muddy waters of the Missouri. April dusk was settling into the streets of the river town of St. Joseph. The afternoon train of the Hannibal and St. Joseph was late, very late. Far down the track sounded the long, echoing scream of its engine. Then the wavering beam of its headlight split the gathering darkness. The little, puffing locomotive began to slow up.

Before it had stopped, the mail pouches had been thrown into eager hands and the men who received them were hurrying to the Post Office. In that tiny building a slight, quick man walked nervously up and down. Tethered outside, a spirited horse pawed the ground.

It was 6:30 when the man received the pouch for which he waited and ran to his mount. Then hoofs sounded on the river road, and a light beckoned at the landing. Men shouted as horse and rider came aboard and the little ferry boat bore into the rippling, high water of the Missouri. As the boat scraped the western bank the rider raced his horse ashore. The boatmen watched them as they hit the rough trail to the west, watched until galloping horse and leaning rider had been swallowed up by the chilling darkness. The first east-west pony express rider was on his way.

In little cabins on the long trail men waited — and women, too — for the sound of a running horse. Food was hot in the kettles. Relay horses were led out to be ready for the quick transfer of saddle and pouch. The nervous, thin relay riders listened anxiously, ran out to look up the trail.

Another rider had started that day from the shores of the

The Pony Express

Another rider had started that day from the shores of the Pacific. A boat had borne him and his horse to Sacramento. There he had begun the first lap of the long ride to St. Joseph. The converging riders were setting a pattern for the day to come. The United States mail would cross the continent faster than the people of the nation would believe possible. Ten days, six hours and thirty minutes — and the mail from St. Joseph was in San Francisco, nearly two thousand miles away. The east-bound rider covered the first twenty miles with one change in fifty-nine minutes. Others sped a hundred and eighty-five miles — crossing the Sierras in thirty feet of snow — in fifteen hours and twenty minutes. The west-bound riders raced from Granada to Seneca to Marysville; Plum Creek to Pat Mullaly's; Alkali Lode to Diamond Springs; South Bend to Three Crossings and Big Smoky. The flat plains and the cotton-wood groves were gone. From the barren land rose sage-brush hills. Hoof-beats echoed in the steep and rocky canyons. They made no sound in the wide, treeless valleys and among the sand dunes. And then the lush green, the yellow sunlight of California!

A stage-coach passenger, Mr. Samuel Clemens, in the days when the swift mail service was running on schedule, wrote down his impressions of seeing the Pony Express rider go by. Later he put them into a book called "Roughing It" and he signed the book "Mark Twain":

★

We had a burning desire from the beginning to see a pony rider. . . . Presently the driver exclaims, "Here he comes!" and every neck is stretched further and every eye strained wider. Away across the dead level of the prairie a black speck

281

appears against the sky and we can see that it moves. In a second or two it becomes a horse and a rider, rising, falling, rising, falling, sweeping toward us nearer and nearer till soon the flutter of hoofs comes faintly to the ear. In another instant a whoop and a hurrah from the upper deck of our coach, a wave of a rider's hand but no reply, and horse and man burst past our excited faces and go winging away like the belated fragments of a storm.

Four hundred gallant horses — Black Billie and American Boy, Muggins and Ragged Jim — brought in the mail with Indian arrows sticking from their sides, with riders up or riders lost from their backs. And eighty riders — Johnnie Frey, Pony Bob Haslam, Wash Perkins, Billy Fisher, Uncle Nick, Si McCandless, Lafayette Bobwinkle, Wild Bill Hickock — it is a roll of honor too soon forgotten. Let one of them tell you how it was when he rode the trails, William Frederick Cody, once known to every American boy as Buffalo Bill, inventor of the Wild West Show:

★

As I was leaving Horse Creek a party of fifteen Indians jammed me in a sand ravine eight miles west of the station. . . . My mount was a California roan pony — the fastest in the stables. I dug the spurs into his sides and lying flat on his back I kept straight on for Sweetwater Bridge, eleven miles distant. . . . The Indians came on behind. . . . I had a lead. . . . When I reached the station, there I found I could get no new pony. The stockleader had been killed by Indians during the night. All his ponies had been stolen and driven off. I kept on therefore to Plont's station twelve miles further along, riding the same pony. . . . At Plont's I told the people what had happened at Sweetwater Bridge. Then with a fresh horse I finished my route.

The completion of telegraph wires across the continent made the Pony Express unnecessary. But before it ended its brief career of a year and a half, riders and horses had written a deathless chapter in the history of the United States mail.

Today our couriers of the air fly the route in fewer hours than the number of days the Pony Express took to cover it. Now as then the spirit is the same — from the pilot winging his way above the mountains to the postman on his daily rounds of the American homes he knows so well. Each bears in mind and acts upon the words that we have so long associated with our mail service.

*

Neither snow nor rain nor heat nor gloom of night stays these couriers from the swift completion of their appointed rounds.

SONGS

The Star-Spangled Banner

THE NATIONAL ANTHEM has become a part of our very lives. And yet "The Star-Spangled Banner" has not been that as long as most of us think. For though the song has been official in the Army and the Navy for more than a generation, it was not officially designated by Congress as the National Anthem until March, 1931. Before that it was one of our national songs. Now it is the one we all acknowledge and honor.

Let us go back to that crucial night in September, 1814, when the American who first called our flag the Star-Spangled Banner waited in dread that the flag would come down under enemy bombardment before the dawn of another day. In 1814 every word in the song meant literally what it said. Let us think again of what those words then meant — and so think more deeply of what they mean today.

For this one scripture we would gladly die,
Our eyes fixed on the flag for which it stands;
This is our creed — for all the world to hear.
This is America set to words and music.
You hear it in the cock-crow over farms,
When sudden sunlight gilds the weathervanes.
You hear it in the roar of great machines,
Making our cities shake with prisoned power.

The Star-Spangled Banner

And when stars hang low about our towns,
Shining in place of windows just gone dark,
You hear it once again. This is our song,
Made sacred by the story of its birth,
And let us tell that story not in words
Grown meaningless with use. Bring back to mind
Forgotten men and women too, to share
The glory of that day. And first recall
Eighteen-hundred-fourteen and Washington in flames,
The enemy sailing north for Baltimore,
And a little girl at work upon a flag.
Caroline Pickersgill, fourteen years old,
And looking lost on the spread of that wide banner,
Stand in the light that shines about it still!
Tell as you told it many years ago,
How once in Baltimore you knelt to sew
And with your mother — for your country's sake —
Made us a lasting symbol of our nation.

★

The flag being over-large, my mother was obliged to obtain
permission from the proprietor of Claggett's, which was in
our neighborhood, to spread it out in their malt-house . . . .
I remember seeing my mother down on the floor placing the
stars.

Placing the stars — stars soon to swing
Into the cloud-strewn blue of America's sky,
Where parapets of frowning Fort McHenry
Guarded the city from the approaching foe.

287

SONGS

The poet paced the deck of his little sloop,
Chained fast beneath the enemy flagship's prow.
Beside her — moored in a wide and sullen arc,
Rode frigates of the foe's proud fleet. He knew
Them out of range of Fort McHenry's cannon
And well he knew the guns above his head
Could pound those far-off walls to nothingness.
Then utter blackness settled suddenly.
And he was blind; but this was not for long.
A rocket screamed above his head and flared
Through heavy-hanging cloud and burst in fire,
Lighting the well-loved shore and dearer flag,
The fifteen stars and fifteen bars that blew
In fluting curves along the rising wind;
Then hundreds of rockets streaking the sky,
And bombs breaking above the distant fort
In waves of sound that hushed the nearing thunder.

Hour after hour they rained upon the fort,
While its brave men stood hopeless to their guns,
Knowing they could not reach their ruthless foe,
Lying so snug and safe and far away.
Hopeless? Yes, all but one fiery captain,
John Berry of the Maryland Militia,
Standing beneath that awful storm of lead
And trying to bring back into his mind
Something he once had seen — some sort of image —
A ship aground somewhere — and guns on her.
Then with a sudden shout he called his men
— No time to ask for orders — bade them mount
And follow him along the curving shore.
In frantic haste they galloped down the sand
Until, lying upon her side, they saw

The Star-Spangled Banner

The old French vessel *L'Eole* — and there
Within her gun emplacements saw long guns,
Cannon with range so great their fire could reach
The tall grim ships still pounding at the fort.
Midnight had passed and sudden rain poured down,
Men heaved at the mighty guns and horses strained,
And slowly, surely, out they rolled and stood.
Then came the long haul back, the hurried placing,
The quick, sure loading, and rain-filled light
Broke soft along the sea — enough to aim by.
The first shot hit the gray waves far beyond
The farthest enemy ship, and raised a fountain
White with spray. The second tore the rigging
Of a frigate and dropped it to the deck.
Then, one by one the white sails of the foe
Rose up against the grayness of the sky
And, bellied out with wind, stood out to sea.

The poet stared into the morning mist,
His pencil moving over ragged paper:

*

O say can you see, by the dawn's early light,
What so proudly we hailed at the twilight's last gleaming?
Whose broad stripes and bright stars, through the perilous
       fight,
O'er the ramparts we watched were so gallantly streaming?
And the rockets' red glare, the bombs bursting in air,
Gave proof through the night that our flag was still there.
O say does the Star-Spangled Banner still wave
O'er the land of the free and the home of the brave? . . . .

SONGS

Yes, Key, because Caroline Pickersgill made it,
Because John Berry saved it, the banner
Still flies above the gallant, battered fort.

*

What is that which the breeze o'er the towering steep
As it fitfully blows, half conceals, half discloses?
Now it catches the gleam of the morning's first beam
In full glory reflected now shines on the stream.

The victory is won. And Caroline's flag
Still flies above John Berry and his men.
They can go home now — back to wives and children,
Back to their shops and offices and markets
After their captain speaks this farewell:

*

Gentlemen, the scenes we have witnessed together are engraved on my heart, and as your captain I bid you adieu with
the sincerity of a friend and the more delicate ties of a
brother. . . . If an enemy shall again assail the home of the
free, this company will be found near the flag-staff support-
ing the star-spangled banner with the same zeal, fervor and
constancy, and united by the same fraternal feelings which
so universally distinguished you while under my immediate
command.

The Star-Spangled Banner

I want you to read something. Just a note
I found — an item in a newspaper —
It will not take me long. Yes, here it is:

★

GREAT-GREAT-GRANDSON
OF WAR VETERAN SLAIN

Frank Russell Whittlesey, private of Marines, direct descendant of Captain John Berry, a hero of the War of 1812, was killed in action on Guadalcanal while fighting off a Japanese attack at dawn, September 14th, 1942.

The fourteenth day, when dawn broke on the sea —
A hundred twenty-eight years to the minute
From that glad moment when Berry's guns spoke
And turned the foe's fleet back upon its course,
Leaving the flag a little girl had sewed
To blow forever down the American sky.
The sewing girl, the captain and the poet,
They were the nation's answer long ago,
And young Frank Whittlesey is our answer now.
The four of them are fabric of our dream,
The American dream of truth and justice won.
The poet sang it on his voyage home
The day his little boat, released from chains,
Bobbed gently back across rain-dappled seas;
Sang it into our heart where it abides.
This is his voice, these his eternal words:

291

SONGS

O thus be it ever when freemen shall stand
Between our loved homes and wide war's desolation,
Blest with victory and peace may the heav'n-rescued band
Praise the power that has made and preserved us a nation.
Then conquer we must, for our cause it is just,
And this be our motto — In God Is Our Trust.
And the Star-Spangled Banner in triumph shall wave
O'er the land of the free and the home of the brave.

★ 32 ★

The Battle Hymn of
the Republic

THE men and women who have spoken or written the words which we now call our American Scriptures could not know at the time that their words would reach through the years to us. They knew only that something needed to be said, and that there was something in their hearts to say. So they said it—then.

Whenever that was, there were many other men and women writing and speaking, that same week, that same day. The words of most of them turned out to be like crops that are eaten the year they are grown, or like flowers that, however charming, live only for a season. But not the American Scriptures. For wherever there are free people, with a right to utter free words, now and then certain words magically take lasting form, and pass from person to person, and from age to age. We do not know just how or why this happens. But it does happen. And it may happen anywhere, at any time, in any circumstances.

Here is a story about the place and time and circumstances which produced one of our Scriptures. It was late in 1861, in the city of Washington.

A party of visitors had come there from Boston. One of them was the daughter of a New York banker named Ward, who had married a Boston teacher of the blind named Howe. Julia Ward Howe had been married for eighteen years. In those years she had had six children, published two volumes of verse and two of prose, written a play, and helped her husband edit a magazine. Recently he, and she so far as she was able, had been giving much of their time to work for the Sanitary Commission — which was the Red Cross of that day.

They had come to Washington to find out how they might best serve their country in this dangerous month of November. Washington was in a tumult. The Union troops, advancing into Virginia in July, had been routed at Bull Run. Ladies and gentlemen from the capital had driven out in carriages to watch the battle, as if it were a picnic. It was not. And there had been dark confusion in Washington ever since. Though the Confederates had not yet attacked the Federal capital, they had strong forces beyond the Potomac. The Union Army was not yet ready for another advance, nor was the Federal government organized for a war.

There was plenty of resolution in the North, but also plenty of indecision and dissension, and in Washington powerful forces pulled this way and that. There were intolerable delays and increasing anxiety. Who could be sure that the United States, the most promising democracy in all history, would survive this conflict?

The visiting Bostonians met the new President from Illinois. Abraham Lincoln seemed to one of them to have great patience, but nothing else. The woman of our story noted only that he said *"heered"* when he should have said *"heard."* They were troubled at the thought that there was so much to be done, and they were able to do so little. The husband had years ago gone, like Lord Byron, to fight with the Greeks for freedom against the Turks; but now he was sixty. The wife was discouraged at the thought that she was useless at a time like this.

But years later Julia Ward Howe was to tell the story of what she then did:

★

I thought of the women of my acquaintance whose sons or husbands were fighting our great battle; the women themselves serving in the hospitals, or busying themselves with the work of the Sanitary Commission. My husband . . . . was beyond the age of military service, my eldest son was but a stripling; my youngest was a child of not more than two years. I could not leave my nursery to follow the march of our armies; neither had I the practical deftness which the preparing or packing of sanitary stores demanded. Something seemed to say to me, "You would be glad to serve, but you cannot help any one; you have nothing to give, and there is nothing for you to do." Yet, because of my sincere desire, a word was given me to say, which did strengthen the hearts of those who fought in the field and of those who languished in prison.

We were invited, one day, to attend a review of troops at some distance from the town . . . we returned to the city slowly, of necessity, for the troops nearly filled the road. . . .

To beguile this rather tedious drive, we sang from time to time snatches of the army songs so popular at the time, concluding, I think, with

"John Brown's body lies a-mouldering in the ground,
His soul is marching on."

The soldiers seemed to like this, and answered back, "Good for you!" Mr. Clarke said, "Mrs. Howe, why do you not write some good words for that stirring tune?" I replied that I had often wished to do this, but had not yet found in my mind any leading toward it.

I went to bed that night as usual, and slept, according to my wont, quite soundly. I awoke in the gray of the morning twilight, and as I lay waiting for the dawn, the long lines of the desired poem began to twine themselves through my mind. Having thought out all the stanzas, I said to myself, "I must get up and write these down lest I fall asleep again." So with a sudden effort I sprang out of bed, and found in the dimness an old stump of a pen which I remembered to have used the day before. I scrawled the verses almost without looking at the paper. I had learned to do this when, on previous occasions, attacks of versification had visited me in the night, and I feared to have recourse to a light lest I should wake the baby, who slept near me. I was always obliged to decipher my scrawl before another night should intervene, as it was legible only while the matter was fresh in my mind. At this time, having completed my writing, I returned to bed and fell asleep, saying to myself, "I like this better than most things that I have written."

When Julia Ward Howe woke again, and looked at her scrawled verses, she found she had written, on the back of a

The Battle Hymn of the Republic

sheet of letter paper, the poem we all know today as "The Battle Hymn of the Republic":

*

Mine eyes have seen the glory of the coming of the Lord:
He is trampling out the vintage where the grapes of wrath
      are stored;
He hath loosed the fateful lightning of his terrible swift
      sword:
  His truth is marching on.
I have seen him in the watch-fires of a hundred circling
      camps;
They have builded him an altar in the evening dews and
      damps;
I can read his righteous sentence by the dim and flaring lamps:
  His day is marching on.
I have read a fiery gospel, writ in burnished rows of steel:
"As ye deal with my contemners, so with you my grace shall
      deal;
Let the Hero, born of woman, crush the serpent with his heel,
  Since God is marching on."
He has sounded forth the trumpet that shall never call
      retreat;
He is sifting out the hearts of men before his judgment-seat:
O, be swift, my soul, to answer him! Be jubilant, my feet!
  Our God is marching on.
In the beauty of the lilies Christ was born across the sea,
With the glory in his bosom that transfigures you and me;
As he died to make men holy, let us die to make men free,
  While God is marching on.

★ 33 ★

Home Sweet Home

ONE of our American Scriptures is very American and is at the same time universal. It is a song. The words were written by an American poet, then living in Paris, and for more than a century they have been sung around the world. The song is "Home, Sweet Home," the words of which are by John Howard Payne, and the music by the English composer Henry Rowley Bishop:

John Howard Payne, young American actor and playwright, looking down from the small round windows that gave scant light to his rear attic room in a Paris lodging-house, saw the quadrangle of the Royal Palace on a bright day in 1822. There fountains lifted little rainbows into the sunlight, bands blared gay music, children danced. But John Payne's mind and heart were on other scenes, and he sat in the half-light to write of them. The words he set down then are among the most treasured of all words. The simple sentences of "Home, Sweet Home" are written on the hearts of millions of Americans who paint with the warm colors of remembrance pictures of the dear days of the not-so-long-ago.

Men love this song — but do not forget it was written for a woman's voice and out of the memory of women, the memory of a soft-voiced, dark-haired mother — lovely Sarah Isaacs, whose father had built the old house Payne remembered as home long before the American Revolution; the memory of Lucy and Anna, two loving and admiring sisters;

the memory of his little cousin, Clari, who had been just his own age and his constant playmate. She died when they were eight years old. But home is more than father, mother, sisters, brothers, friends. Home is things as well as people.

Beside blue Atlantic waters the south shore of Long Island rises into the rolling Shinnecock hills. Just at their foot the old fishing village of East Hampton sleeps in soft and salty air. You go down a long, elm-shaded street, past the still clear pond at the fork, and there you see it — a simple house, shaped like an old-fashioned salt-box. It would seem too rigid and severe if it were not for the vines that clamber over its walls; the white picket-fence covered with honeysuckle and rambler roses; the sun-dial waiting out the time it measures; the curving, gray windmill still groaning round and round as the ocean winds blow on. You can tell, somehow, that children have lived there.

A house like this is a memory of children. It is a history too intimate, too dear for strangers. But we Americans are not strangers. The story of a house like this is the story of all our old houses. So let us read the letter John Howard Payne wrote home from across the ocean to his sisters, Lucy and Anna:

*

My yearnings toward home become stronger, as this term of my exile lengthens. I long to see all your faces and hear your voices. 'Twould do me good to be scolded by Lucy and see Anna look pretty and simple and sentimental. I feel the want of you — parts of myself — in this strange world. I long for home about me. When they told me in days of yore I had a double crown to my head and should cross the seas, I thought it is a fine thing to get away from home to old countries. Not on account of the twin coronals though. One crown is more than I hope will ever be at home in our country. Living among kings gives one a great respect for countries when a man governs only because a whole nation deems him worthy.

Out of such remembrance John Howard Payne built his song. Legend has it that a slow tune was sounding in his ears as he wrote — a tune he had heard while walking through the fields of Italy. A peasant girl, carrying a basket laden with flowers, was singing it — and he stopped her and begged her to sing it again while he wrote down the plaintive air.

He was remembering someone else, too, as he wrote — his little cousin-playmate Clari — now dead more than a score of years — but so close had been the bond between them that he had chosen to adapt the musical drama "Clari, or the Maid of Milan" for which he was writing the English words — chiefly because it bore her name.

"Clari" was produced for the first time in London on a night in May. The English actress, Anna Marie Tree, dressed in trilled white muslin, played the part of Clari, and sang the words into the heart of the world.

Many great singers sang it afterwards. Adelina Patti, one of the greatest sopranos who ever lived, sang it once — back in the 1860's — at the White House. She had ended her concert and was about to give a last encore when tall, ungainly, bearded Abraham Lincoln rose from his chair and walked to a small stand beside the piano. He took from it a music book with a vivid green cover, and placed it on the piano-rack, opened to the music of "Home, Sweet Home." Then he went back to his seat without a word. When the song ended the

Home Sweet Home

President and Mrs. Lincoln were in tears, and Adelina Patti wept, too, remembering that they had recently lost their beloved son, Willie.

The Lincolns were not thinking of the White House then, but of a house in Springfield, Illinois, where Willie was born. Wherever the words of this song have been heard they have conjured up in the minds of their hearers pictures of home. And homes are as different from each other as the people who listen. "Home," said a living poet, the greatly loved Robert Frost, "is something you somehow haven't to deserve." We know millions who deserve it now — millions who have fought for it and sing John Howard Payne's song — each with a different image in his heart. Yet somehow all the pictures blend into one great vision — the vision of free America, our homeland.

★

Mid pleasures and palaces though we may roam,
Be it ever so humble, there's no place like home;
A charm from the sky seems to hallow us there,
Which, seek through the world, is ne'er met with elsewhere.
 Home, Home, sweet Home!
 There's no place like Home!
 There's no place like Home!
An exile from home, splendor dazzles in vain;
O, give me my lowly thatched cottage again!
The birds singing gaily, that come at my call,—
Give me them,—and the peace of mind, dearer than all!
 Home, Home, sweet Home!
 There's no place like Home!
 There's no place like Home!

★
ACKNOWLEDGEMENTS
★

The publishers wish to express their appreciation to: Marshall Davidson, of the Metropolitan Museum of Art, for his invaluable help in the selection of the pictures; A. Hyatt Mayer, also of the Metropolitan Museum of Art, for his many valuable suggestions; to the many institutions and individuals who have so generously granted permission to reproduce their pictures. The publishers are also indebted for permission to include the following copyrighted material: *Nancy Hanks* by Rosemary Benet (from: *A Book of Americans,* published by Rinehart & Company, Inc. Copyright, 1933, by Rosemary and Stephen Vincent Benet) *John Brown's Body* by Stephen Vincent Benet (from: *Selected Works of Stephen Vincent Benet,* published by Rinehart & Company, Inc. Copyright, 1927, 1928) *Buffalo Bill's Life Story* by William F. Cody (published by Rinehart & Co., Inc. Copyright, 1920) *The Campers at Kitty Hawk* by John Dos Passos (from: *The Big Money,* by permission of the author) *The Death of the Hired Man* by Robert Frost (by permission of Henry Holt & Company) *Lincoln, The Man of the People* by Edwin Markham (by permission of Virgil Markham) *Ann Rutledge* by Lee Masters (by permission of the author) *Flag Day, 1940* (by permission of the *New York Times*) *The Naturalization of Jack Roberts* (by permission of Random House, Inc.) *Davy Crockett* by Constance Rourke (by permission of the publishers, Harcourt, Brace & Company. Copyright, 1934).